PREPARING STAFF TO SERVE PATRONS WITH DISABILITIES

A How-To-Do-It Manual

Courtney Deines-Jones
Connie Van Fleet

HOW-TO-DO-IT MANUALS
FOR LIBRARIANS

NUMBER 57

NEAL-SCHUMAN PUBLISHERS, INC.
New York, London

Published by Neal-Schuman Publishers, Inc.
100 Varick Street
New York, NY 10013

Library of Congress Cataloging-in-Publication Data

Deines-Jones, Courtney.
   Preparing staff to serve patrons with disabilities : a how-to-do-it
manual / Courtney Deines-Jones, Connie Van Fleet.
      p.   cm. — (How-to-do-it manuals for libraries ; no. 57)
   Includes bibliographical references and index.
   ISBN   1-55570-234-1 (alk. paper)
   1. Libraries and the handicapped—United States.   I. Van Fleet, Connie
Jean, 1950– . II. Title. III. Series.
Z711.9.H3D44   1995
027.6'63—dc20
[025.1'976'63]   95-31958

CONTENTS

FIGURES

PREFACE

Different measures of disability define disability in different ways, but most are in general agreement over the number of people who are affected by a disability. The figures reported here are drawn from a 1992 survey of disability as reported in *Morbidity and Mortality Weekly Report*, v43 n10 (October 14, 1994) p730(5).

An estimated 35-49 million Americans over age 15 have some form of disability. This means that almost one in five people in the U.S. has problems performing daily activities without help. The number of people in the U.S. who have disabilities is likely to grow for a number of reasons. The American population is aging, and people over age 65 have the highest incidence of disability. Medical technology is increasing the chances of survival for infants with severe disabilities. And at the same time, health care is becoming more expensive and public funding for health care is decreasing, putting children at risk for birth defects. Compounding the situation, aid to poor children and families is being cut, which may lead to more developmental defects for this group.

In the past, a rise in people with disabilities might not have had a large impact on library staff members. Many people with disabilities were restricted because of a lack of transportation, discriminated against by a lack of educational opportunities, and kept from full interaction with other people because of prejudice and communication barriers. This situation is changing, however. Technological advances are creating new opportunities for the print disabled, and laws such as the Americans with Disabilities Act (ADA) are helping to ensure that all people, regardless of disability, are able to participate to the fullest extent possible in all aspects of life. Children with disabilities are far more likely to attend regular public schools, and people with disabilities of all ages and walks of life will rightfully expect the same library services as their peers.

The importance of library services to people with disabilities cannot be overestimated. People with disabilities have the same information needs as any other segment of the population, but often require innovative strategies to access that information. The challenge of providing excellent service to all patrons, including those with disabilities, is paramount to fulfilling the library's mission. As important as physical access to facilities and services is the environment in which the library provides those services. With the passage of the ADA and subsequent improvements in physical plant accessibility and access to transportation, libraries are serving increasing numbers of patrons who have some type of disability and, for the reasons noted above, these numbers should continue to increase for some time.

If your library serves 100,000 people, 5,000 probably have difficulty using or traveling to the library because of a disability. If your library serves a large number of senior citizens or is located in a poor community, the number of people who cannot benefit from standard library services will be even larger, perhaps approaching 20 percent of the patron base.

Most library staff members are caring people who want to serve all of their patrons, including those with disabilities. Unfortunately, many library staff members are poorly trained to meet this challenge. Others, unaccustomed to serving these patrons, may feel

Professional associations can help people who want to improve service. Associations sponsor workshops, produce bibliographies and brochures of useful information, and provide a network of concerned colleagues who can help point a program in the right direction and give encouragement when spirits are low. Some professional organizations include:

Association of ADA Coordinators (AADAC) One World Trade Center, Suite 800, Long Beach, CA 90831-0800, Voice/Relay 800-722-4232; Fax 800-932-9232.

American Library Association (ALA) Sections, Committees, and Groups 50 East Huron St., Chicago, IL 60611, Voice (ALA Headquarters) 800-544-2433, TDD (ALA Headquarters) 312-944-7298, Fax (ALA Headquarters) 312-280-3255; 3256; 3257; 3258.

Library Service to Children with Special Needs Committee *Association for Library Service to Children (ALSC), ALA,* contact: Association for Library Service to Children, Voice (ALA Headquarters), ext. 2163, Voice (Direct) 312-280-2163.

Association of Specialized and Cooperative Library Agencies (ASCLA), ALA, For all groups associated with the ASCLA, contact: Voice (ALA Headquarters), ext. 4399, Voice (Direct) 312-280-4399.

Americans with Disabilities Act Assembly*Association of Specialized and Cooperative Library Agencies (ASCLA), ALA.*

Library Service to the Blind and Physically Handicapped Forum (LSBPHF) *Libraries Serving Special Populations Section (LSSPS), ASCLA, ALA.*

Library Service to the Deaf Forum (LSDF) *Libraries Serving Special Populations Section (LSSPS), ASCLA, ALA.*

Library Service to the Impaired Elderly Forum (LSIEF) *Libraries Serving Special Populations Section (LSSPS), ASCLA, ALA.*

Library Service to Developmentally Disabled Persons (LSDDP) *Libraries Serving Special Populations Section (LSSPS), ASCLA, ALA.*

Library Services to People Who Are Mentally Ill *Libraries Serving Special Populations Section (LSSPS), ASCLA, ALA.*

Academic Librarians Assisting the Disabled (ALAD) *Libraries Serving Special Populations Section (LSSPS), ASCLA, ALA.*

Adaptive Technologies Interest Group *Library and Information Technology Association (LITA), ALA,* contact: Library and Information Technology Association, Voice (ALA Headquarters), ext. 4270, Voice (Direct) 312-280-4270.

Library Service to Young Adults with Special Needs *Young Adult Library Services Association (YALSA), ALA,* contact: Young Adult Library Services Association, Voice (ALA Headquarters), ext. 4391, Voice (Direct) 312-280-4391.

Friends of Libraries for Deaf Action (FOLDA) contact: Friends of Libraries for Deaf Action, PO Box 50045, Washington, DC 20004-0045.

uncomfortable and awkward, again compromising service standards. And a few staff members may have stereotypical attitudes about people with disabilities which may make them insensitive to patron needs.

This book is designed as an aid to serving people with disabilities. Rather than addressing management concerns such as restriping parking spaces or hiring interpreters, this book covers the day-to-day operations of the library, providing tips, resources, and procedures front-line staff can use to help provide excellent service to non-traditional patrons. The emphasis is on practice, as opposed to policy, and stresses easy and inexpensive ways to improve the library environment for all patrons.

We have developed this book as a ready reference tool as well as an aid to staff development. Consequently, chapters are organized the way libraries are, by service areas. We have also added sections on the special considerations of both youth and senior services, staff development, and library safety.

The importance of staff attitudes and expertise in providing a climate of service excellence cannot be overstated. The best policies will be effective only if they are implemented by well-trained, knowledgeable staff members who are comfortable serving all types of patrons. This book recognizes that importance, and helps both library managers and staff prepare to meet the challenge of serving non-traditional patrons with disabilities.

RESOURCES

Black, J.B., Janet Black, Ruth O'Donnell, and Jane Scheuerle. *Surveying Public Libraries for the ADA*. Developed and printed for the Pinellas Public Library Cooperative. May 1992.

This is THE BEST single source we have encountered for basic guidelines for compliance with the Americans with Disabilities Act. It provides checklists, background, and tips for implementation. Copies were distributed to state libraries, or contact the Bureau of Library Development, Division of Library and Information Services, 500 S. Bronough Street, Tallahassee, FL 32399-0250.

Foos, Donald D., and Nancy C. Pack, eds. *How Libraries Must Comply with the Americans with Disabilities Act (ADA)*. Phoenix, AZ: Oryx, 1992.

In one of the first books focusing on library compliance with the Americans with Disabilities Act, Pack and Foos gather essays covering a range of issues related to the act. Included are chapters on history of relevant legislation, explanations of basic elements of the law, and planning for compliance.

Velleman, Ruth A. *Meeting the Needs of People with Disabilities: A Guide for Librarians, Educators, and Other Service Professionals*. Phoenix, AZ: Oryx Press, 1990.

This update of Velleman's original book (*Serving Physically Disabled People: An Information Handbook for all Libraries*) is an excellent reference source in providing services to people of all ages. Encyclopedic in scope, it contains a comprehensive listing of individual and agency service providers as well as important information on accessibility and service issues.

Walling, Linda Lucas, and Marilyn H. Karrenbrock. *Disabilities, Children, and Libraries: Mainstreaming Services in Public Libraries and School Library Media Centers*. Englewood, CO: Libraries Unlimited, Inc., 1993.
Although this book focuses on services to children, it is an invaluable source in understanding the nature of various disabilities and their effects on the way in which patrons use library materials and services. This is a fairly dense book, containing a wealth of information that is organized in a clear and useful manner.

1 LIBRARY ORIENTATION AND INSTRUCTION

Patrons get a sense of a library from the instant they walk through the doors. Do you acknowledge them, or allow them to wander about until they look hopelessly confused? Are you willing and able to introduce new patrons to the library, or do you stay behind the force-fields of your information desks? Does your library have a prepared, systematic orientation, or does the quality of a tour depend entirely upon who is giving it?

Although initial contact is important to all patrons, it is especially important to patrons with disabilities. Patrons with mobility or visual impairments need to know about barriers and obstacles before they reach them. Patrons with difficulty using certain bibliographic aids need to know if the library has special equipment and where it is located. And if some facilities are not accessible to patrons with mobility or other impairments, they need to know that up front, to avoid wasting valuable time in fruitless attempts to get needed information.

Reactions of well-meaning staff members who are unprepared to serve patrons with disabilities can fall to two extremes. On the one hand, some will hesitate to offer help to library users who have disabilities out of fear of being thought of as patronizing or overbearing. On the other hand, they may be solicitous to the point of being stifling.

Library managers and staff members should make every effort to balance these two extremes in providing a consistently excellent introduction that serves the needs of all patrons while remaining sensitive to the concerns of patrons with disabilities. Every library should develop a standard orientation procedure which can be followed by any staff member. The formality of library orientation programs will naturally vary widely, but the basic elements of programs are the same. A good program must meet a minimum of three goals.

- Anticipate patron needs. This eliminates the need to rush around frantically when a non-traditional patron visits.
- Introduce basic bibliographic aids such as patron catalogs. If a library is too large to manage adding this component in a general tour, separate bibliographic orientation sessions should be available to new library users.

- Recognize that not all disabilities are readily apparent. The orientation program should always indicate where adaptive equipment and facilities are located, and where patrons needing additional help can receive assistance.

By consistently following the same inclusive orientation program, and ensuring that additional help is available for patrons who need a more intensive introduction to the library, you will be prepared to assist patrons with disabilities as effectively and pleasantly as possible, making the introduction to the library a positive, low-stress experience for everyone involved.

ETIQUETTE FOR SERVING PATRONS WITH DISABILITIES

- Approach a patron with an offer of help, but wait until the offer is accepted.

- Do not pass judgment on the validity of a patron's statement of disability. Remember that disabilities are often invisible. Many people do not appear to have disabilities even though they do.

- Remember that while people who use wheelchairs or who are of short stature may have difficulty reaching high shelves, patrons with other disabilities may find it very hard to bend down to reach low shelves.

- Do not touch wheelchairs or mobility aids without permission. Leaning or hanging on a wheelchair is an invasion of personal space. Moving a wheelchair or crutches may leave a person stranded.

- When patrons ask you to act as a guide, offer your elbow. Do not grab arms or push patrons; instead, allow them to hold on and follow you.

- When giving directions to people with visual or mobility impairments, be very clear and include information on distances, changes in floor level, and any obstacles along the way.

- Remember that a disability is not an illness. Do not treat people with disabilities as though they are sick.

- Don't be offended by a lack of response or unconventional behavior. People with hearing impairments may not have heard or understood you; other disabilities may affect social or motor skills, causing unusual responses.

- Remember that using a mobility aid such as a wheelchair or walker is not in itself a tragedy. Mobility aids give people the freedom to move about independently.

- Do not pet or play with guide dogs or working animals. These animals are not regarded as being just pets and distracting them can put their owners in danger. Always ask permission of the owner before interacting with an animal.

- Always let the people with the disabilities decide what they can and cannot do. Do not neglect to mention programs or services because you think patrons with disabilities would not benefit from them.

- Interact with patrons who have disabilities as you would with any other patrons. Remember always to think of the person first.

ANTICIPATING PATRON NEEDS

The most important moment of service to patrons with disabilities is the moment of initial contact. "Should I help her, or will it look patronizing?," "What should I say to him?," and "How should I behave?" are typical questions many staff ask when meeting people with disabilities for the first time. By anticipating patron needs, you can go a long way toward preparing yourself for this initial contact and be comfortable welcoming any patron into the library.

It is, of course, impossible to anticipate the needs of every single patron who will ever walk into a library. With proper advance work, however, it is possible to meet the vast majority of those needs. You can then look forward to meeting non-traditional patrons with anticipation, rather than with dread. A few basic reminders will help ensure you're ready.

- Keep maps of the library on hand at all times.
- "Police" public areas to check for wayward chairs, step stools, or other impediments to traffic.
- Practice using all library equipment, including equipment which has been modified for use by people with disabilities.
- Review the basics of etiquette for serving patrons with disabilities. Share stories and successful service techniques with other staff, and don't be afraid to ask questions!

Preparing the Physical Environment

If the library is not physically accessible to people with disabilities, the best service in the world will not improve access. Most of the decisions affecting physical accessibility will fall to management, but access does not end at the doorway or with the architect's plans. For example, the 36" aisle space mandated by the ADA helps nobody when that space is blocked by carelessly pulled-out chairs, potted plants, holiday signs, step stools, and the like. By making it a habit simply to clear aisles and push in wayward furniture, each staff member can help make the library environment much more inviting, and safer.

One person should walk through the library at least twice a day to make sure accessible walkways, stacks, and other areas are clear of obstructions. This person should be sure to check:

- wheelchair accessible reading and study areas (make sure chairs are not blocking accessible spaces and workstations);

Figure 1.1 DAILY FACILITY ACCESS CHECKLIST

Branch/Section: _____

Check each area of your department or branch to ensure that walkways are clear and that there are no obstructions to access by people with disabilities. Note any problems you cannot correct and bring them to the attention of your supervisor or division head.

✓ **Item**

_____ Doorways are clear and doors open easily

_____ Floors are dry, carpet is flat, edges of rain/snow mats are flush with the floor

_____ Floors are clear of trash and debris

_____ Book trucks, step stools, plants, displays, etc. do not block accessible routes, facilities, or areas

_____ Furniture is in place with chairs pushed in

_____ Wheelchair accessible areas are not blocked by chairs or other furniture

_____ Signage is clear, accurate, and not blocked

_____ Banners, displays, etc. hang no lower than 80" from the floor where people walk

_____ Protruding objects do not extend into or block accessible routes

_____ Accessible workstations and adaptive aids are working

_____ Adaptive equipment stored at the desk is in place

_____ Hazardous areas are clearly marked from all accessible sides

Any other access concerns?

Date:_____   **Time:**_____

Surveyed by:_____

- all aisles, stacks, and passageways;
- restrooms; and
- entryways and security gates.

A complete daily checklist, modified to include elements appropriate to your library, can serve as a written reminder and as a tool to identify chronic problem areas. Where there are problems, staff members can prepare for and plan around them, keeping service levels high.

COMMON PROBLEMS

PROBLEM: The library has areas which are inconvenient or impossible for some patrons to get to.
SOLUTION: Know where these areas are and which parts of the collection are housed there. Offer immediate assistance when patrons wish to use these materials. Don't send them off to discover the problem alone.

PROBLEM: The library is large, and the people who sit at the information desk do not know which materials are accessible and which are not.
SOLUTION: Integrate information on accessibility into the look-up sheets at the information, circulation, or reference desks. A bright sign saying "CONSTRUCTION IN MUSIC ROOM!" or the like can be taped to the desk or terminal as a reminder of areas which may be temporarily inaccessible.

PROBLEM: Self-guiding photocopied maps are left out for patrons, but are too small to write in all the areas which are or aren't accessible.
SOLUTION: Highlight maps and information sheets to indicate accessible routes and inaccessible areas. Use light blue (the "color" of accessibility) to mark accessible routes, restrooms, or special facilities. Use yellow or orange to indicate areas which may not be accessible. Be sure to include a statement in large print telling patrons where they can get assistance if they need help.

Welcoming Etiquette

You can start off on the right foot by remembering some common-sense etiquette tips.

- Maintain a "person first" attitude. Accept people with disabilities as individuals. Listen to what patrons are saying. Don't assume you know what they want or what's best for them.
- Use signage to indicate that people with disabilities are welcome and to direct them to appropriate service points. Many patrons like to use the library independently and clear signage will help them to do so.
- Be natural. Smile, nod, and speak as you would to a patron without a visible disability. Do not speak in exaggerated, overly enthusiastic, or overtly sympathetic tones.
- Be flexible. Patrons are individuals who require you to use a variety of skills to interpret questions and provide answers.
- Use the same effective listening and interviewing techniques that you already know. Waiting for an answer, using minimal encouragers, checking understanding through paraphrasing or restatement, and asking questions are techniques you probably use every day.
- Be sensitive to language that supports negative stereotyping. People use wheelchairs to provide transportation and freedom of movement, they are not "wheelchair bound." But don't worry about using colloquial expressions such as "see you later" to a blind person or "let's run along" to a person who uses a wheelchair.
- Make eye contact. Look directly at the person to whom you are speaking. Try to have your heads at approximately the same level. If your interview with a person who uses a wheelchair lasts more than just a few moments, pull up a chair.

Staff members who are concerned that they will not "say the right thing" to patrons with disabilities may end up saying nothing. You will not have this worry if you simply welcome patrons with disabilities as you would any other patron. A simple "may I help you" is never in poor taste. Nor is it improper to offer help to any patron who is having trouble negotiating a doorway or lifting a heavy book sack.

Remember, though, that the offer is just that, and accept a "no, thank you" with grace. If there is any concern that patrons do not know assistance is available, go up to them and tell them directly. Do not follow patrons around "just to make sure" there is no need for assistance. There is nothing more disconcerting than being stalked through the library by a surreptitious staff member, no matter how good the intentions behind the action are.

Because staff members are not always free to greet each new patron individually, post a sign at the entrance or on the front desk offering assistance.

PROBLEM: A staff member greets a patron, but is ignored.
SOLUTION: There are two possibilities: that the patron chose to ignore the offer of help, or that the patron did not hear the offer. If eye contact was not established during the initial exchange, the staff member should attempt to draw the attention of the patron or move into the patron's line of sight and re-issue the offer. Remember, though, that patrons may ignore greetings for any number of reasons. If you have made a reasonable attempt to get the patron's attention and there is no acknowledgment, let it go at that.

Preparing Attitudes

Having a positive attitude before meeting patrons is perhaps the single most important step to providing excellent service. Develop a positive attitude by asking questions such as "What would I do if a person using a walker came in to use the library?" Mentally rehearsing such scenes will make everyone more comfortable with their ability to help all patrons.

Take an attitude self-evaluation survey to help identify areas of conflict or tension. After taking the quiz, review it question by question, using these guidelines.

1. People with disabilities create a lot of problems for libraries.

   - It is important to distinguish between legislation and individuals. Many librarians are intimidated by the ADA, but have found their interactions with individual patrons to be pleasant and rewarding. Some have also found that people with disabilities are a demanding litigious lot. In fact, people with disabilities are individuals, and you will find that their personalities are as varied as those of most of your patrons. Don't generalize about all people with disabilities from your experience with a few.
   - Library staff have had to evaluate library services in terms of the ADA. In some cases, they have had to make significant physical renovation or adaptations in service.
   - Most accommodations have been fairly low cost and many libraries have used grant money to minimize impact on local budgets.
   - The ADA and national focus on people with disabilities have stimulated libraries to examine their missions and to reach a new or previously underserved client group.
   - Staff training focused on services to people with disabilities has improved staff skills and service provision for all library users.

Figure 1.2 CHECK YOUR AWARENESS

Listed below are some common ideas about library service for people with disabilities. This exercise is intended only to help you examine your own ideas and attitudes and to serve as a basis of discussion.

Yes   No

____   ____   1. People with disabilities create a lot of problems for libraries.

____   ____   2. Accommodations for people with disabilities cost a lot of money and benefit only a few people.

____   ____   3. People with disabilities have a hard time and deserve special treatment.

____   ____   4. Deaf people would really like to be able to hear.

____   ____   5. I am embarrassed to try to serve a person with a disability.

____   ____   6. People with emotional disabilities are dangerous and should be kept out of the library.

____   ____   7. The number of people with disabilities will probably decrease in the future due to advances in medical technology.

____   ____   8. People who are blind or physically handicapped get all the library service they need from the National Library Service for the Blind and Physically Handicapped.

____   ____   9. Librarians have a higher level of tolerance toward people with disabilities than does the population at large.

- How has the focus on people with disabilities affected your library? Have there been positive and negative effects?

2. Accommodations for people with disabilities cost a lot of money and benefit only a few people.

- Most accommodations have been fairly low cost (under $500); many involve service accommodations rather than physical renovation.
- Accommodations incorporated into initial building are far less expensive than renovations in established buildings.
- Accommodations have been found to benefit a wide range of library users. Older patrons, those with invisible disabilities or temporary disabilities, parents with young children in strollers, and staff all benefit from ramps and elevators. Materials related to disabilities are useful not only for people with disabilities and their families, but for professional caregivers, community agencies, and private businesses that are now courting people with disabilities as consumers. Books on tape are popular with commuters, people for whom English is a second language, and beginning readers as well as for people with visual and learning disabilities. Everybody benefits from clear, readable signage and instructions.
- What has been the monetary cost of some of the accommodations made in your library? Which patrons have you noticed making use of accommodations?

3. People with disabilities have a hard time and deserve special treatment.

- Most people with disabilities don't consider themselves victims and don't want your pity. Most people with disabilities don't consider themselves heroes and don't want your admiration. They have simply adapted as most people adapt.
- The ADA is about using accommodations to provide equal service, not privileged service. While patrons with disabilities may require some accommodations, they should not be given preferential treatment. For instance, people with disabilities should not be moved to the front of lines. If a person is using crutches, you might offer the person a place to sit while waiting for his or her turn.
- Would I rather have pity or respect? Have I recognized

the abilities and accomplishments of individuals with disabilities?

- What sorts of services would I consider to be accommodations, and what sorts would I consider preferential treatment?

4. Deaf people would really like to be able to hear.

- Some deaf people would like to be able to hear, but many deaf people feel a strong sense of identity with the deaf community. The deaf community has its own language and culture. Many members do not consider deafness a disability. They consider people who are not able to communicate through their language (sign language) to have a disability.

5. I am embarrassed to try to serve a person with a disability.

- Embarrassment is a natural reaction when people are placed in a social environment in which they are uncertain of the rules of behavior.
- Some people are genuinely afraid of hurting a patron's feelings through inept or inappropriate responses.
- As people interact more with people with disabilities, they begin to recognize them as individuals and to feel more comfortable in relating to them.
- What do I need to know to feel more comfortable in providing service to people with disabilities? Am I more comfortable around some people than others? Why?

6. People with emotional disabilities are dangerous and should be kept out of the library.

- Most people with emotional disabilities are indistinguishable from the average person.
- Most people with emotional disabilities represent no threat to anyone.
- Historically, people with emotional (mental) illness are subject to greater superstition and fear than people with most other types of disability because their behavior is perceived of as unpredictable and because the causes of illness are not understood.
- Libraries should have policies in place to deal with people who exhibit threatening behavior, whether that behavior is due to emotional illness or not.

- Do I regard all people with emotional disabilities as "problem patrons"? Can I distinguish dangerous or problem behavior from behavior that is unconventional but harmless?
- Do I know the library's policy on defining and dealing with threatening or potentially violent behavior?

7. The number of people with disabilities will probably decrease in the future due to advances in medical technology.

- The number of people with disabilities has not decreased due to advances in medical technology. Some experts suggest that advances have led to an increase in people who survive serious disability or illness resulting in a disability.
- Diagnostic techniques have aided in identifying people with disabilities at an earlier age. Many disabilities not previously recognized, such as attention deficit disorder or some types of learning and perceptual disabilities, are being recorded in greater numbers than ever before.
- Environmental factors, such as pollution, alcohol or drug abuse, and poor prenatal care, affect more newborns than genetic factors and the effect of these factors appears to be growing.
- Does the number of people with disabilities make a difference to the library's commitment? Have I noticed more people with disabilities in the community?

8. People who are blind or physically handicapped get all the library service they need from the National Library Service for the Blind and Physically Handicapped.

- The National Library Service for the Blind and Physically Handicapped offers excellent service for people who are not able to use traditional print materials and are unable to visit the local library on a regular basis.
- Many people with disabilities function well within the community and prefer a more integrated approach that allows them to use the services of the local library.
- Local libraries offer more varied and complete service than the National Library Service (NLS). Programming, reference service, and local materials are more readily available at the local library, as is the opportunity to interact with other community members.

- What does the NLS offer? What does it provide that is superior to what we have locally? What does the local library provide that can't be provided by the NLS? Why would someone prefer to use the local library? Are there groups that the local library serves that the NLS does not?

9. Librarians have a higher level of tolerance toward people with disabilities than does the population at large.

- A series of research studies indicate that librarians, as a group, tend to have higher tolerance for people with disabilities than does the population at large. The studies also indicate, however, that librarians follow the same value pattern as the general population. They are most accepting of a person with only a moderate disability of one sense (hearing or seeing) and least accepting of people with developmental disabilities.
- Retail outlets and businesses have begun to focus on people with disabilities as new consumers. Note the number of ads featuring people with disabilities that have appeared on television or in print media. Next time you go shopping, look for signs that businesses are developing accommodations that make it easier for people with disabilities to spend their money.
- What do you think of the results of the surveys? Do you share in the attitudes that the researchers found?
- What are the implications for libraries as more and more community and business services are made available to people with disabilities? Does it seem right for the Wal-Mart to be more interested in service than the library? Will this interest influence the type and amount of consumer information we make available?

If you work in a small library or do not have people in-house with whom you can discuss service incidents, consider joining an Internet Listserv devoted to issues of library access. Some appropriate Internet Listservs are listed in Chapter 2.

If you run into difficulty providing service to patrons, review each incident with other staff members and brainstorm ideas for improving service in the future. An outline of a service incident review form (p. 14) can help ensure that relevant points are covered in an informal manner. The key is to ensure that all discussions are:

- comfortable,
- frank,
- non-judgmental, and
- solution-oriented.

Talk through actual experiences, examine strong points in service provision and stress ways in which service could be improved. Follow the form and quit when you are finished. These sessions, when conducted in a safe environment and focused on the goal of service provision, will keep attitudes positive. Everybody should be encouraged to contribute ideas, no matter how far-fetched they may sound at first, and nobody should be censored for their opinions. The objective is to improve service, not to evaluate individual employee performance.

Is It Catching?

Despite all medical evidence to the contrary, many people, some of whom work in libraries, fear that they can "catch" certain disabilities from patrons. This is especially true with patrons disabled by the effects of HIV/AIDS.

HIV can only be transmitted by an exchange of body fluids. It cannot be transmitted by handling books or materials which have been used by an infected person. It cannot be transmitted by using the same computer equipment as an infected person. Further, it cannot be transmitted by casual contact, such as an orientation tour or reference interview.

Some staff members may ask to wear gloves when serving patrons with disabilities, or will refuse to get close to these patrons. If you choose to wear gloves while working, you should do so at all times. It is highly offensive to don protective clothing when working in a casual library setting just because patrons are thought to have a certain disability or disease.

GIVING DIRECTIONS AND CONDUCTING WALK-THROUGHS

New patron orientation should include a facility tour, especially for patrons with disabilities. But because not all patrons will attend formal library tours, the library should provide plenty of maps in the largest print possible. Libraries which serve many people who have visual impairments may also wish to have a 3-D scale model of each floor built to help guide patrons. Models are also useful if the library is spread among several buildings.

Maps are useless, however, if they are outdated or unclear. Informational maps should always be made using the same standard guidelines.

- Depict each library floor on a separate piece of paper.
- Ensure maps and models are to scale. It is worth the money to have a set of masters made from blueprints or floor

---

Figure 1.3 SERVICE INCIDENT REVIEW FORM

Use this form when completing written reports about service provision or as a guide to discussing improvements in service quality.

Describe the patron's problem or concern.

What was done to try to help?

Did this satisfy the patron? If not, what other ideas were tried to meet the patron's needs?

Was the patron satisfied with the solution to the problem? Why or why not?

Was the patron satisfied with the service they received? Why or why not?

What suggestions, if any, did the patron make for improving future service in this area?

Was the staff member satisfied with the solution to the problem? Why or why not?

What steps could staff members take to improve service in similar situations?

If you can't afford a model of your library, consider making a low-cost tactile map.

1. Photocopy a plan of the building or floor onto a transparency or thin piece of paper. Be sure to use a plan that is drawn to scale and use the largest size available.

2. Tape the copy face down onto a sheet of tagboard on a soft surface, such as a pad of construction paper or a soft blotter. To prevent tearing, tape just the edges or use removable tape.

3. Using a ruler to keep lines straight, trace the map with a stylus or dried-out ballpoint pen. Then, using a stencil, label it. Be sure to write the letters and labels backwards!

4. Turn the tagboard over and make sure all the lines and letters are clearly raised, without tears. Do any touch-up necessary.

5. Use a Braille labeller or a stylus to add Braille legends and labels.

plans. Even if furniture or shelf arrangements change, the basic elements of the building will still be to scale and the map will be easy to update.

- Clearly indicate different functional areas of the library, circulation and information desks, rest rooms, meeting areas, and emergency exits. If possible, use color coded maps.
- Identify accessible entrances and facilities using the universal symbol of accessibility. The universal symbol of accessibility is used to designate parking spaces, entrances, and facilities which are wheelchair accessible. Adding access symbols to maps can prevent frustration for patrons who use wheelchairs.

- Clearly mark accessible routes. This is imperative when some routes are not accessible. Be sure to indicate ramps, elevators, and other accessible features.
- Do not clutter the map. It is not necessary to indicate every individual book stack and rack, so long as the functional areas and accessible routes are clearly marked. Excess detail can make labels difficult to read, especially for patrons with visual impairments or perceptual disorders.
- Update the map as collections shift or areas are rearranged.

In addition to paper maps, libraries should have oral "maps" to guide patrons through the facility. Many larger libraries offer taped self-guided tours as a standard library orientation aid. A special orientation tape will help patrons who have visual impairments. In addition to the location of basic functional areas of the library, this tape should include the following information:

- Exact locations of features including distances involved;
- Location of stairs, changes in terrain, or other obstacles detailed as precisely as possible;
- Locations of Braille controls and signs;
- Locations of adaptive equipment; and
- Locations of help desks.

If at all possible, this tape should be scripted by somebody familiar with providing such information. State and non-profit rehabilitation agencies or schools for people with visual impairments

Color-coding maps is a good job for young volunteers or community service workers when the library cannot afford color photocopies or a color printer. Staff members can also color-code maps when there are slow times at reference, information, or circulation desks.

Making a map may seem foolish in a tiny library, but for some people, even remembering locations in a small area is very difficult. A map saves the patron from having to ask repeatedly where certain things are. It also helps when pointing out collection locations to patrons who do not communicate orally or who have difficulty understanding directions. Even one-room libraries will benefit from a handout which indicates doors, basic facilities, and major collection locations.

may be willing to produce a tape tour free of charge for your library.

Armed with this good map, offer to give new patrons a tour of the facility. When patrons use mobility aids, such as wheelchairs or crutches, treat the aid as an extension of the patron's body. Do not push a wheelchair or "steer" a person unless asked to do so. If there is a particularly difficult area to negotiate, issue a warning and offer to help, but be willing to take "no" for an answer. Most people with disabilities can navigate through an accessible library without any trouble if staff members follow a few basic rules of etiquette.

- When escorting patrons who do not communicate orally, bring paper and pencil along so that questions can be asked and answered as they arise.
- If blind or visually impaired patrons request guidance, offer your elbow and lead by it. Be sure to announce upcoming obstacles and whether stairs and ramps are going up or down. If other people join the conversation, announce their presence. If you must leave for some reason, announce this as well.
- Give very specific instructions when directing blind patrons. For example, "go five feet/meters/yards straight ahead, then turn right. The elevator is on the right-hand side, and the control buttons are to the right of the elevator," is much better than "just go down the hall and it's on your right."
- When patrons are accompanied by personal aides or interpreters, be sure to address yourself directly to the patrons.
- Point out library features while keeping the disability in mind. If certain areas are not physically accessible or if they require adaptive equipment to be used, be sure to say so and to indicate the service desk at which patrons may get help.

HELPING PATRONS WITH DEVELOPMENTAL DISABILITIES OR MENTAL IMPAIRMENTS

Most patrons with disabilities can benefit from a standard library orientation program. For some patrons, however, this approach is not appropriate. Many people who have developmental disabilities or mental impairments need individualized orientation to the library, followed by guided repetition and practice. Others may simply be unable to use bibliographic searching tools or to translate the information they get from a search to an actual shelf location. Following some general guidelines will help improve library orientation for patrons who cannot benefit from a standard tool because of mental impairments.

- Try to arrange to help patrons individually or, at the very least, in small groups.
- Conduct the orientation in small chunks geared to the patrons' actual needs. For example, do not start teaching the Internet to patrons who only want to locate books in the library's collection.
- Keep language, both spoken and written, clear, simple, and concise. Remember that both reading and language comprehension levels may be low.
- When repeating instructions, use the same terms and procedures. Changing expressions or language may confuse patrons, as will demonstrating a number of alternative ways to access the same information.
- Encourage patrons to ask for help when they need it, and be sure they know where the nearest help desks are. Do not leave patrons until you are sure they understand how to find the information they want and how to get any help they may need.
- Treat people with developmental disabilities or mental impairments with respect. Adults with these disabilities should be treated as adults, not children.

EXPLAINING BIBLIOGRAPHIC AIDS

Library orientation tours often indicate the catalog simply as "right over there," offering little more instruction in how it is used. For patrons with disabilities, these tools may be nothing more than frustrating barriers to the collection. People with dyslexia may transpose call numbers and never find the books they need. Patrons with visual impairments may not be able to read the type on the screen or on the card in the drawer. And those with limited hand motion may find moving a computer mouse or flipping individual cards nearly impossible.

Library staff members who introduce patrons to the library should be sure to include information about and demonstrations of bibliographic tools. Adaptive aids and equipment should be pointed out and demonstrated, and any rules for checking out these items should be fully explained. Explaining bibliographic aids is important whether the finding tools are in a computerized or print format.

While you should keep the disability in mind, do not neglect to point out materials just because you think certain patrons will not be able to use them. Patrons are the ones who are best able to determine whether or not they will benefit from specific materials or formats.

On-Line Tools

Screen magnifiers, voice recognition software, and modified interfaces are becoming more common and less expensive all the time and, consequently, more libraries are taking advantage of these tools. At libraries which use any of these aids:

- All staff members who come into contact with the public should be trained to use them.
- Terminals which have enhancements should be clearly identified and their location should be shown on all informational maps.
- Because many people have "invisible" disabilities, staff members should always indicate which terminals are equipped with adaptive technology when giving orientation tours.
- Orientation should include a brief session using the on-line catalog. This can include information on basic search strategies, using any adaptive equipment, and obtaining help if needed. The orientation should, whenever possible, be conducted using an accessible terminal to demonstrate features such as screen magnification, whether or not a member of the tour group "looks" as though she/he has a disability.

Some libraries have different types of computerized bibliographic aids (for example, CD-ROM stations and OPACs). Be sure to let patrons know if the adaptive equipment differs among types of workstations. Let patrons know what type of aids are available at each station, and point out the location of the service desks nearest each station.

Card Catalogs and Printed Finding Aids

Card catalogs can be difficult tools to use for patrons with disabilities. Often, people looking through the catalog block the aisles, making access for patrons using mobility aids nearly impossible. Unthinking patrons may leave used drawers on top of the catalog, above the reach of people who use wheelchairs. The little golf pencils and scraps of paper used to write down citations are also often stored on top of the catalog, again inaccessible to patrons with limited reach height.

Even if they can get to the catalog, some patrons may have trouble flipping through cards, or deciphering the information contained on them. People with visual impairments and some types of learning disabilities may have special concerns when attempting to use the card catalog or any printed bibliographic tool.

Always give out handouts when conducting instructional tours. Use a separate handout for each finding tool, describing its basic operation. Keep extra copies near the computers, indexes, or card catalogs for ready reference by patrons and staff.

During the orientation tour, point out alternative locations of scrap paper and pencils, lower tables to which catalog drawers may be taken for browsing, and the location of the nearest service desk where patrons may ask for help. Tell patrons how they may borrow hand magnifiers or other aids if they are needed.

There is a great temptation to assume that with the advent of computerized information, no patron would ever want to use the paper index except under extreme duress. Some people, however, may find using a printed index causes less strain than using a computer terminal. If bibliographic tools such as magazine indexes are available in both printed and computer forms, the locations of both should be indicated during orientation.

Incidental Equipment and Facilities

Orientation tours often neglect important non-collection elements such as rest rooms, copy machine locations, snack areas, smoking lounges, or other facilities. Whenever these exist, they should be included as part of the basic orientation. Accessible rest room and lounge facilities should be indicated as a matter of course, and the location of service desks indicated for those who may need assistance operating equipment.

CONCLUSION

By remembering that all patrons have varied needs and preparing appropriate tools and aids in advance, you should be able to conduct successful orientation sessions with almost all patrons. The result is likely to be library users who have formed a favorable opinion before even opening a book or keying in a search command. At the same time, you will be more relaxed and comfortable introducing yourself and the library to all patrons, including those who have disabilities.

RESOURCES

Norlin, Dennis A. "We're Not Stupid You Know: Library Services for Adults with Mental Retardation." *Research Strategies* 10, no. 2 (Spring 1992): 56–68.
Norlin describes his study of a library instruction program for patrons with mental retardation. The findings will be useful to those providing services to this group.

Norton, Melanie J. "Effective Bibliographic Instruction for Deaf and Hearing-Impaired College Students." Pages 118–150 in *Libraries Serving an Underserved Population: Deaf and Hearing-Impaired Patrons*, ed. by Melanie J. Norton and Gail L. Kovalik. *Library Trends* 41 (Summer 1992).
Norton traces the legislative background mandating services to people with

disabilities, describes bibliographic instruction techniques to use in group instruction and individually, and supplies copies of materials used at the Wallace Library (Rochester [New York] Institute of Technology).

Systems and Procedures Exchange Center. *Library Services for Persons with Disabilities*. SPEC Kit 176. Washington, D.C.: Association of Research Libraries, 1991.
This kit, which contains reprints of documents from a number of universities, is an excellent resource for all types of libraries. Included are planning documents, service policies, staff training materials, building evaluation plans, and brochures and handouts. Particularly useful are etiquette guides (such as "What Do You Do When You Meet a Blind Person?") that have been synthesized from brochures developed by national associations of people with disabilities.

Wright, Kieth C., and Judith F. Davie. *Serving the Disabled: A How-To-Do-It Manual for Librarians* No. 13. New York: Neal-Schuman Publishers, Inc., 1991.
Wright and Davie provide a fine, practical manual. Geared primarily to managers, it provides important background information and addresses policy issues and administrative concerns at the organizational level.

2 READER'S ADVISORY AND REFERENCE SERVICES

One of the most essential tasks of front-line library staff members is guiding patrons to the information they need. From the initial reference interview to the final selection of material, you help patrons focus their topics, determine where resources may be found, and examine alternatives which will maximize the library's effectiveness in finding needed information. Providing reference and reader's advisory help to patrons with disabilities can present special challenges, especially when there are communications barriers between patrons and staff. Providing information in alternative formats can also be a difficulty, especially in smaller libraries which may lack the means to purchase text readers and other adaptive equipment.

The goal of any library should be to provide equal access to services and information to all patrons, regardless of disability. To provide this service sometimes requires us to go the extra mile, and can involve some cost. With proper planning and a little creativity, however, this goal can often be met even by people working in tiny libraries on tinier budgets.

COMMUNICATIONS BARRIERS AND TECHNIQUES TO OVERCOME THEM

Communications barriers are often the most frustrating of all. Patrons who cannot make staff members understand their needs may become frustrated and angry. This, in turn, makes staff members more defensive and less likely to be able to listen to what patrons are trying to say. Library managers can help by taking some simple steps at service desks to make communication easier.

- Make sure the counter is well lit, so that patrons can clearly see staff members' faces. This makes communication with people who read lips or rely on facial expressions much easier.
- Ensure all service desk printers have covers. The reduction in noise level can be significant.
- Keep an ample supply of reasonably sized scrap paper (half-sheet or larger) on hand. If written communication is necessary, it is best not to have to conduct it on bookmark-sized bits of paper.

When you have difficulty understanding patrons and must ask them to repeat themselves, be sure to indicate that you believe the fault lies with your comprehension. Some polite ways to request clarification:

"I'm having a difficult time understanding. Would you mind repeating that?"

"I'm sorry, but would you mind writing that down?"

"Could you please spell that for me?"

When you are having a hard time understanding, it is especially important to repeat the patron's request so that you are sure you have it right.

- If possible, mount computer monitors so that they may be swiveled toward the patron. Showing the information as you go is very useful in many situations.

Trouble-Shooting Typical Communications Problems

PROBLEM: The patron does not respond when addressed.

SOLUTION: The patron may be deaf or hearing impaired. Attempt to attract attention by gently tapping on the counter or waving your hand in the patron's line of sight. (Do not, though, signal frantically in the patron's face.)

PROBLEM: The patron has difficulty understanding staff members.

SOLUTION: If the patron reads lips, ensure that the lighting is adequate, and especially that there is no backlighting. Enunciate clearly, but do not speak loudly or too slowly, as this tends to distort the mouth.

SOLUTION: Do not chew gum or eat at the desk. Keep hair, hands, pencils, etc. from blocking your face.

SOLUTION: Try speaking in a different tone of voice. Certain types of hearing loss only affects certain registers, and speaking in a lower or higher tone may help the patron better understand. This is especially true if the staff member's natural voice is very high or very deep. Again, be sure to enunciate clearly, but do not shout or speak too slowly.

SOLUTION: If the patron is wearing an assistive listening device and indicates that you should speak into it, go ahead. Again, speak clearly and in a well-modulated tone without shouting.

SOLUTION: Try speaking in clearer sentences. This does not mean resorting to a kind of babied-down pidgin. Instead, construct sentences without long dependent clauses, use the clearest terminology possible (no library jargon or acronym "everybody knows"), and leave out irrelevant information.

SOLUTION: If all else fails, write it down. While written communications at the reference desk do not have to be in full sentences, they should be complete and cogent. Cryptic notes will serve the patron no better than cryptic conversation.

PROBLEM: The staff member doesn't understand the patron.

SOLUTION: Re-state to the patron what you believe was said and ask for confirmation and expansion as necessary. This may take some time if the patron has a disability which severely affects speech.

SOLUTION: Be patient. Allow the patron to completely finish a thought or sentence. The natural tendency to want to jump in and provide a word to someone who is having problems speaking should be curbed at all cost. The word you want to supply may be wrong.

SOLUTION: Enlist the aid of another staff member. People have different "ears" for language. A sentence which seems completely incomprehensible to one person may be perfectly clear to another.

SOLUTION: Remain calm. Anxiety will only decrease your ability to communicate. Remember that you are not in a race. The important thing is to help the patron, and if it takes a few minutes more, nothing is lost.

SOLUTION: Ask the patron to write it down. Be sure that the piece of paper you hand the patron is larger than 2" x 4".

PROBLEM: The patron is aphasic, using the wrong words when trying to convey a concept.

SOLUTION: This rare situation has the potential of being extremely frustrating to both parties. Try getting at the desired topic by asking increasingly focused questions which require only basic answers. The patron may also do better by writing the request.

PROBLEM: The patron uses an interpreter for communication, and the staff member isn't sure who to face when listening and responding.

SOLUTION: Face the patron. If, for some reason, you are addressing the interpreter him- or herself, then do look at the interpreter, but be sure that your face can still be seen by the patron.

PROBLEM: Tall service counters are a barrier for patrons who are of short stature or who use wheelchairs.

SOLUTION: Come out from behind the desk and, for conversations of any duration, attempt to place yourself at about the same eye level as the patron. It is better to accompany the patron to an accessible terminal and provide help there where everyone can see what is going on than to stay behind a counter which blocks the line of sight.

TELEPHONE INFORMATION SERVICE

Telephone information services are heavily used in all libraries and represent some patrons' only contact with the library. This is especially true for patrons who lack the means or the ability to come to the library themselves. Library information services range from automated informational and story tapes to personalized reference service, and it is in personalized reference service that staff members will have the most contact with patrons.

Because of advances in telecommunications technology, libraries may be able to communicate with patrons who are using personal computers, telecommunications devices for the deaf (TTYs and TDDs), or faxes. Always remember that the standard for service is that people with disabilities should have the same access to information as people without. This may mean delivering information through faxes or scanners rather than holding information at the desk for people with disabilities who find it difficult to get to the library. Such services may be provided free to people with disabilities, even if there is normally a charge. Staff members should be aware of policy and supported by it. It is the responsibility of management to ensure that appropriate and workable policies are in place.

If your library experiences problems with non-disabled people taking advantage of such specialized service intended for those with disabilities, consider keeping a "permission sheet" verifying the patron's eligibility to use the service, much the same way as the National Library Service for the Blind keeps applications on file to ensure services are delivered to those who truly need them. The verification sheet may also contain information on the types of equipment the patron uses to receive information to help reference staff members when answering requests.

Text Telephones and Relay Services

Telecommunication devices with automatic printouts cost less than $500 and should be within the reach of almost any library. These text telephones plug into standard modular jacks and can be configured so that both a voice and a text telephone share the same incoming line. They allow patrons to communicate directly with the library, and therefore provide the same privacy and one-to-one contact a voice telephone offers. One nice thing about a text telephone with a printer is that it provides a written record of the call, so that the staff member does not need to be writing down title and author requests as they scroll across the screen.

USING YOUR TDD

Punctuation

Do not use any punctuation when typing. Not all TDDs are compatible in the way in which they interpret punctuation, and you may end up having to re-type your message.

Commonly Used Abbreviations

GA—Go ahead. When you have finished typing your message, press "GA" to let the other person know they can start. When reading a message, wait for the GA before you start typing.
GA TO SK—Go ahead if you need to; I am finished. This indicates the typist is finished with what is to be said in the call. It is more polite than SKSK, as it gives the other party a chance to respond before hanging up.
SKSK—Hanging up. Use this to indicate you are disconnecting the call.
HAHA—Indicates laughter.
HD—Hold.
PLS—Please.
Q—Question. This is often used instead of "?" because it is easier to type.
SMILE—Indicates that a statement was meant (or taken) as humor.

Receiving a Call

Type a polite greeting which identifies the party the caller has reached. If you have one TDD which serves all library departments, a simple HELLO THIS IS THE PLEASANTVILLE LIBRARY GA is sufficient.

Remember to wait for the patron to type GA before beginning your responses, and to end your responses with a GA.

Placing a Call

If using an acoustic coupler, place the mouthpiece to the left. If you are calling a line which is combination voice/TDD, set your TDD's announcer on. Let the phone ring for a longer time than you would for a voice call. When the other party answers, begin your conversation.

Be sure to identify yourself and the person you are trying to reach immediately. A sample introduction might be HELLO THIS IS DIANNE FROM THE PLEASANTVILLE LIBRARY I AM CALLING FOR MR JOHN SMITH IS HE AVAILABLE Q GA.

Ending a Call

Try to end with pleasant words. If the patron types kind words, add a simple YOURE WELCOME or SAME TO YOU before typing SKSK and hanging up. Be sure to disconnect the line or hang up the receiver once the call is finished.

Three guidelines will help ensure optimal use of your TDD.

- Everybody who would possibly answer a voice call should be trained to answer a text call as well. If there are text telephones at more than one branch in the system, staff members can practice by occasionally calling one another.
- Tape a "crib sheet" next to the phone or on the phone itself (see page 25) listing how to perform basic operations and specifying the signaling terms used in text communications.
- Put the text telephone in an area that is staffed during all library hours, rather than at a secondary station which may not always be attended. Because in many libraries the text telephone is rarely used, library managers may decide to put it in an out-of-the-way place with the ringer turned up loudly enough for people at the main reference station to hear. The problem with this set-up is that when a call does come in, the reference desk staff members must stop what they are doing, rush across the library, and start using an unfamiliar piece of equipment. Frustration on both ends of the conversation is likely to seriously compromise service quality.

Relay Service Etiquette

Talk to the patrons, not the operator. Say "How can I help you?" not "Ask him how I can help him."

Do not make side comments to others while you are talking. The relay operator will transcribe anything you say, and if you start talking with others, your TDD conversations are likely to become garbled.

If you must interrupt your calls, ask patrons if they mind being put on hold. If they prefer, arrange to call back through the relay service. Remember to get their TDD phone numbers before signing off.

At libraries or branches too small to have a text telephone, the staff members can still communicate with deaf patrons through a relay service. Available now in all 50 states, relay services offer toll-free communication between text telephone users and any other voice telephones in the state. Deaf patrons make calls through a centralized relay service, using their text telephones. An operator at the relay center then completes the call to the voice telephone, and acts as an interpreter throughout the conversation, converting text to voice and vice versa. The system may also be used by people with voice telephones who wish to contact someone who uses a text phone.

A major drawback to a relay service for many librarians is that it requires a third person to listen in on the reference conversation. But the service is free, and may be the only option a tiny library has to communicate with text telephone users. If your library or branch uses a relay service, be sure to brief staff members on its use. It is particularly important to note that when staff members are making outgoing calls to text telephones, they must have phone numbers for the patron's text telephone as well as for the relay service. Without this information the relay operator cannot place the call.

Whether using a text telephone or a relay service, it is important to conduct the conversation naturally, just as you would with a voice call. Clarify the patron's request, provide the information needed, and ensure that the patron has understood the information. After answering a few text telephone calls, staff members will feel far more comfortable using the equipment, so during the early stages it is important to have this task distributed among many employees so that one person does not become "the" text telephone reference librarian.

Making Time for the Patron with a Disability

PROBLEM: The library is understaffed, and people are at a premium. It is difficult for a staff member to spend significant amounts of time with any one patron. A patron arrives who needs significant help finding information.

SOLUTION: Go to the subject area with the patron. If the books are too high or too low for the patron to reach, get a full-size book truck (half trucks may pose a danger if they can be easily tipped over) and place books for the patron to browse on it. Remember, however, not to simply reproduce the shelf conditions (e.g., if the patron cannot stoop, do not put books on the bottom shelves of the book truck).

SOLUTION: Give the patron a periscope so that the titles of books on upper and lower shelves may be viewed. Inexpensive plastic periscopes can add a few feet to a patron's range of vision. This may be enough to allow the patron to browse the collection independently.

SOLUTION: If the patron is browsing unbound or unboxed magazines or paperbacks, provide a "grabber." These devices can extend a person's reach by two or three feet, enough to get high or low materials, eliminating the need for staff members to page these items. They should not be used for retrieving books, however, because of the risk of pulling down a book (or shelf of books!) onto the patron's head. If your library uses grabbers, a warning to this effect should be taped to the grabber, and staff members should also be instructed to tell patrons that the grabbers are for magazines and paperbacks only.

SOLUTION: Schedule a time for the patron to come in when the library is most likely to have staff members free to help. Although the library may not as a rule allow patrons to schedule time with staff members, when serving people with disabilities this is a minor courtesy, especially given the extra effort they may have to make to arrange transportation to the library.

SOLUTION: Include patron assistance as one of the job duties of volunteers. Volunteers or scheduled staff members who have a good command of language and pleasant speaking voices may also be able to help serve patrons with impairments who need to have information read to them.

SOLUTION: If your library has adaptive equipment, be sure that everyone who works with the public understands how to use it at least on a basic level. Otherwise, patrons may have to depend on being lucky enough to come to the library when the one person who knows how to work the machinery happens to be on duty. This is unfair to patrons and may present problems for the library if the knowledgeable person leaves or wants to take a vacation.

No matter how much planning and streamlining the library does, there will be certain patrons who monopolize staff members' time. This happens with patrons who are not disabled, too, and staff members should be sure they are applying standards evenly for everybody. It is a good idea for libraries to have some sort of flexible policy in place for in-house assistance just as they do with telephone assistance. For example, a policy that employees may only spend a maximum of 15 minutes at a time with any individual patron when other patrons are waiting for service ensures that the patron will get a reasonable amount of assistance while giving an impersonal means of terminating the session if there are other patrons who need help.

READER'S ADVISORY FOR PATRONS WITH DISABILITIES

Many people like to read about people with whom they identify. Readers also want books about people who share their heritage and experiences, as is evidenced by the growing number of books targeted toward specific racial, ethnic, and religious groups. It is logical to assume that the same is true for people with disabilities. But just as not every Catholic wants books about priests and not every Hispanic craves novels about Hispanics, not every person who is visually impaired wants to read books with blind characters.

SOME MAJOR LIBRARY OF CONGRESS SUBJECT HEADINGS RELATED TO DISABILITY

Many libraries classify both fiction and non-fiction work using Library of Congress subject headings. Some of the current subject headings related to disability are listed below.

Afro-American handicapped
Children of handicapped parents
Communication devices for the disabled
Computers and the handicapped
Developmental disabilities
Developmentally disabled
Handicapped (has many subdivisions and narrower terms)
Handicapped children (also has many subdivisions and narrower terms)
Handicapped-owned business enterprises
Handicapped parents
Handicapped teenagers
Handicapped women
Handicapped youth (has several subdivisions and narrower terms)

Hispanic American handicapped
Indians of North America—handicapped (also used as a subdivision for other groups of Native Americans)
Libraries and handicapped children
Libraries and the handicapped
Mentally handicapped
Parents of handicapped children
Physically handicapped
Reading disability
School libraries—services to the handicapped
Teachers of handicapped children
Veterans, disabled
Wages—Handicapped

Staff members should have access to bibliographies of books by and about people with disabilities (some sources are listed later in this chapter). But the reader's advisory interview should proceed exactly as it would for any patron. If a blind patron remarked that she loved historical straight British mysteries, it might be appropriate to suggest Bruce Alexander's *Blind Justice*, which casts Sir John Fielding (who was blind himself) as the detective. If the same patron had expressed a fondness for hard-boiled detective stories, on the other hand, this would not be a good recommendation. The important question the reader's advisor should ask is "would I recommend this book to this patron if disability were not an issue?" Only if the answer is yes should the book be offered. It does the patron a disservice to recommend a second-rate or otherwise inappropriate book just because the character has a disability which matches the patron's. This practice should be strongly discouraged unless the patron specifically requests a book by a certain author or with characters who meet specific demographics.

Format

Until recently, books were issued in one format. Increasing demand, however, has led to a trend in which books which are sure to be best-sellers are simultaneously issued in regular print, large print, audio CD, and cassette versions. Large print books are losing their dowdy image and being packaged in brighter colors, often with the same dust jackets as the regular print editions.

Each format has its own strengths and weaknesses which should be taken into account when selecting material; no "one" format is best for everybody. The strengths and weaknesses of common formats are discussed below.

"Regular" Print Books

This is still the most common form in which new books are published. "Regular" print, though, may vary widely, and some of these books are in a font large enough to satisfy large print readers.

Strengths of regular print books:

- Ready availability, especially for new or less popular works.
- Variable typeface and layout schemes mean that some may be accessible to people who normally need a large print format.
- No stigma attached to their use.

Drawbacks of regular print books:

- No typeface standards; it is impossible to tell in advance whether a book will be typeset generously or in a cramped, hard to read face.
- Some British books reach the U.S. large print market before they do the small print market.

Paperbacks

Paperback books sell in large numbers, but people often do not think of them in connection with service to patrons with disabilities. They do have some qualities, however, which make them the right choice in certain situations.

Strengths of paperbacks:

- Light weight makes them easier to use for some people who have limited hand and arm strength or who like reading in bed.
- Inexpensive and ephemeral; can often be bought at a low

cost by the library, and can be circulated in cases in which damage is likely or return doubtful.
- Preferred format for many young adults and older children.

Drawbacks of paperbacks:
- Bindings often refuse to stay open, making reading difficult for those who cannot hold both pages apart.
- Typeface and layout can be small and cramped.
- Pages may yellow, reducing contrast.
- Binding quality may be low; books may easily fall apart.

"New Reader" Books

SELECTION CRITERIA FOR NEW READER BOOKS

- **Topics:** of interest to the age group and ability level for whom they are selected. Adolescents and adults will want informational books on dating, health, and occupations. Sports, romance, humor, action, adventure, current events, and popular biography are popular. Condensations and adaptations of best selling authors are good bets for adolescents and adults.
- **Plots:** clear, straight, uncomplicated story lines are best. Remember that this simplification is often necessitated only by the patron's reading ability, not by level of intelligence.
- **Characters:** should be three-dimensional, fully developed people, not wooden stereotypes.
- **Text:** simple sentence structure and familiar vocabulary. Generally, concrete languages and images are best.
- **Print:** large, well-spaced, dark with good contrast.
- **Length:** short (75 pages is usually the maximum. Many works are much shorter. This will vary with degree of illustration and layout of text.)
- **Graphics:** numerous, well-drawn illustrations. It is important that new reader books for adults be well illustrated, but that they not look like children's picture books.

These slim volumes, usually paperbound, are designed to be used by adults who are learning to read. They contain short stories, condensed novels, and non-fiction works mostly focusing on life survival skills. Some readers only wish to read a novel in its entirety exactly as it was published; but for those who do not mind condensed versions, new reader books are often an excellent choice.

Strengths of new reader books:

- Are specifically designed to offer adult high interest/low vocabulary reading material, and are usually compiled with assistance from literacy professionals.

- Often incorporate narrative passages from the original, allowing the reader to get the "feel" of the author's narrative style.
- Usually have very clear print and typesetting which can be used by large print readers.
- Are low-cost materials.

Drawbacks of new reader books:

- Selection of materials is limited and geared mostly toward a younger audience.
- Paperback format may be difficult for some readers to use.
- Poorly constructed books may fall apart easily.
- Do not present the full text of most works.

Large Print Books

Large print books are probably the most common adaptive text format. With an aging population and more people who can benefit from these books, demand has increased. Now, many major publishers release small and large print versions simultaneously. New, light-weight opaque paper makes it possible to produce a large print book which is not much thicker than its small print cousin, although it may be many pages longer. Material ranging from ephemeral westerns to weighty classics are available in this format, and the industry is expanding to include more young adult and children's works.

Strengths of large print books:

- Easier to read for people with many visual impairments.
- Contain the entire text of a work.
- May offer some British works unavailable in the U.S. in other formats.
- Production quality is usually high.

Drawbacks of large print books:

- Selection may be limited, especially in children's books, non-fiction, and less popular works.
- Older works may be unattractively packaged and may encompass several thick volumes.
- Newer works, while thinner, may be quite heavy.

Large print books typically have a type size from 16 to 20 points, although sometimes an even larger type is used. Font style also has an impact on how large the type appears, so if you are planning a brochure, be sure to see a sample of the font at the correct size before making your final plans.

This is Times New Roman, 10 point
This is Times New Roman, 12 point
This is Times New Roman, 14 point
This is Times New Roman, 16 point
This is Times New Roman, 18 point
This is Times New Roman, 20 point
This is Times New Roman, 24 Point

Books on Tape and Audio Compact Discs

Most libraries have some type of audio collection, and most readers have a tape or CD player in their homes or cars. Audio format materials are consequently an extremely popular alternative format for patrons both with and without disabilities. As with large print books, publishers are recognizing this and are beginning to release popular works simultaneously on tape, often with celebrity readers. Children's books come packaged with both book and tape together. Regular cassette tapes are the most common audio format offered by most public libraries, and these should not be confused with the special audiotapes offered through the National Library for the Blind and Physically Handicapped, which are discussed below.

Strengths of regular audio format materials:

- Are accessible to patrons with very limited or no vision.
- Can be easily used by people with temporary vision loss.
- CD format material is relatively hardy.
- Sturdy, inexpensive tape player availability may make it possible for the library to loan equipment to patrons.

Drawbacks of regular audio format materials:

- Tapes are easily damaged.
- Selection of material is limited, especially for CD format.
- Popular audio editions may be abridged. Of course, this may be a benefit to people with limited attention spans.

- Inaccessible to people who do not own tape players, unless the library loans equipment as well.

Videotapes

Videotapes can be a viable alternative material format and are often overlooked by library staff. Many people own VCRs, and most libraries have at least a small educational video selection which will include some film adaptations of classic plays and stories.

Strengths of videotapes:

- If close- or open-captioned, are accessible to deaf and hearing-impaired patrons.
- Present material in both visual and auditory formats, which may increase comprehension.
- Present material unavailable in print.
- Integrated TV/VCR units enable libraries to lend viewing equipment to patrons.

Drawbacks of videotapes:

- Selection is limited to those works which have been adapted for television or cinema.
- Works may have been extensively modified for film or television adaptation.
- Inaccessible to people who do not own a VCR, unless library loans equipment or allows patrons to view videotapes on-site.

Interactive Compact Discs (CD-ROM)

CD-ROM versions of some adult and children's books are gaining popularity. Adult mystery adaptations are popular, as they allow the patrons to work through the puzzle at their own pace, sometimes from a first-person point of view. Children's books also allow the reader to explore many paths to the final resolution of the story, which may have several possible outcomes. As computer and virtual reality technology become more common, this type of "book" will undoubtedly gain in popularity.

Strengths of CD-ROMs:

- Allow reader to complete the story at any pace and, often, to several different conclusions.

- Children's books often incorporate educational games into format.
- Present material in audio and visual formats, and allow patrons to use their own adaptive electronic interfaces to improve access.
- Read-only CD-ROMs eliminate danger of contamination from viruses.

Drawbacks of CD-ROMs:

- Inaccessible to patrons who do not own a compatible computer, unless the library offers on-site reading workstations.
- May be frustrating to people who simply want to read the story, rather than work though series of puzzles to get the answer.
- Selection is extremely limited.

National Library Service for the Blind and Physically Handicapped

Two formats, Braille and talking books, are not mentioned above because in most cases these will be offered to patrons through the National Library Service for the Blind and Physically Handicapped (NLS). The NLS operates through state libraries to provide special talking book tapes and players to people who have disabilities which make print formats inaccessible. The talking book format is specifically designed for this purpose and is not the same as a regular audiocassette. The NLS also provides Braille books for those who need them.

Public and academic libraries should keep a supply of NLS application forms on hand to distribute to patrons. The form can be certified by a doctor or a librarian; in many cases, the librarian will be able to certify that the patron is unable to use print format material. Once the application has been submitted, the librarian's duties are complete. All material loaned through the NLS will come from the agency through its depository libraries in each state at no charge to the patron.

Public and academic libraries which wish to have material translated into Braille can usually locate a local source for this service, either through their state library's department which serves patrons with disabilities or through a local school for the blind or visually impaired. In many cases, Brailling can be done for free or for a nominal fee. Academic and school libraries are more likely to be involved in this type of work, Brailling assigned course materials.

Read, Read, Read!

The best way for staff members to become good readers' advisors for patrons with disabilities (as for any patron) is to read, read, read. Some libraries have reading plans incorporated into their employee evaluation programs; they should consider requiring that a certain percentage of the books be for or about people with disabilities. Library managers who do not work where reading is required should nonetheless encourage it by sharing book review journals and announcements of forthcoming books with employees, suggesting new books, or having unofficial reading contests. March, which is Disabilities Awareness Month, is a good time to promote books by and about people with disabilities to staff members, who could then develop an annotated bibliography based on their readings for distribution to patrons.

WHERE DOES STAFF RESPONSIBILITY END?

Staff members may feel compelled to provide more than readers' advisory or reference services. Or, they might feel the need to "go the extra mile" for patrons, especially those with disabilities. Overdoing it can cause problems. When these problems arise, staff members must remember where their responsibility ends.

Staff Members Are Not Physicians

PROBLEM: Patrons come to the library expecting to find out which medical treatment is best or asking for an opinion on a miracle cure they saw advertised in a supermarket tabloid.

SOLUTION: Unless they have a current license to practice medicine, staff members must be very careful not to recommend any type of treatment or make any kind of prognosis for a disease.

SOLUTION: Refer the patron to a community group which has that disability or treatment as its focus.

SOLUTION: A staff member may point out that the *New England Journal of Medicine* is more thoroughly researched than the *National Enquirer*, but must stop short of saying that the miracle cure advertised in the tabloid is a sham. If the patron requests the article promoting the miracle cure, and there are articles that have debunked the treatment, the staff member may by all means mention these to the patron, but it is not the staff member's place to make a value judgment.

SOLUTION: Smile sympathetically and say "Well, you'd really have to ask your doctor."

PROBLEM: The staff member has had personal experience with the disability in question and considers him/herself an expert.

SOLUTION: The staff member may refer the patron to a community group, but should not offer medical advice under any circumstances.

Staff Members Are Not Lawyers

PROBLEM: Patrons ask for legal advice or for legal interpretation of the ADA.

SOLUTION: Library staff members who have not passed the bar are not lawyers. The Americans with Disabilities Act (ADA) is not a document which should be interpreted by a public service librarian. Staff member clarifications of the law should be strictly limited to providing definitions, descriptions, cases, and examples contained in the library or gained through library resources.

SOLUTION: Do not attempt to provide your own interpretations. Refer the patron to a community or legal aide organization or suggest contacting a lawyer.

PROBLEM: The staff member has had personal experience with a legal case involving disability and considers him/herself an expert.

SOLUTION: Refer the patron to a community or legal aid organization. Every case is unique. Anecdotal or personal experience with the law is just that, and should not be shared with the patron or used as a basis of making judgments among different courses of action.

Staff Members Are Not Personal Aides

PROBLEM: A patron asks a staff member to administer medication.

SOLUTION: Unless it is a life-or-death situation, don't. If there is an emergency, call 911 and request assistance.

PROBLEM: A patron asks a staff member for help with personal tasks.

SOLUTION: Politely decline. Patrons with disabilities should expect the same access to services enjoyed by all. Sometimes, this requires that a staff member personally assist a patron in paging books, reading information, etc. The staff member is not, however, required to be a personal aide to the patron. As a general rule of thumb, this means that tasks patrons would have to perform in their own homes do not have to be done by the staff member. Examples of such tasks include helping the patron use the toilet, wash up, or get into or out of a wheelchair.

PROBLEM: The staff member is asked to bring water from the fountain.
SOLUTION: If the fountain is not accessible or is not on an accessible route, bring the water.
SOLUTION: If the fountain is accessible, but the library is crowded and the accessible route is congested, deliver the water if possible. This is not required, but is a minor courtesy.
SOLUTION: If the staff member is busy and the accessible route is clear, direct the patron to the accessible fountain.

Responding to Harassing or Dangerous Conditions

It is the library manager's responsibility to resolve problems in a way that will allow the patron to retain the greatest access possible while protecting the rights of staff members. Sometimes, this may mean confronting the situation of a patron with a psychiatric or other disability who is harassing or dangerous to staff members or other patrons. In these cases, library managers must use the same procedures the library would follow with patrons who do not have a disability. Frontline staff members should not be put in the position of making policy decisions regarding any patron's access to materials.

PROBLEM: An adult patron vocalizes inappropriately, disturbing other patrons or staff members.
SOLUTION: Staff members should expect and tolerate the same behavior from a patron with a disability as for one without. However, if staff members routinely ignore infants and children who scream or call out, they should not attempt to censor an adult patron who vocalizes inappropriately because of a disability.
SOLUTION: Ask the vocalizing adult to relocate away from a quiet study area, and provide comparable facilities on the same floor. Try to err on the side of accommodation, going as far as possible to aid the patron.

PROBLEM: A patron's behavior toward a specific staff member is lewd or inappropriate.
SOLUTION: Behave as you would toward any patron. Staff members should not be expected to put up with harassment or abuse from any patron, disabled or not.
SOLUTION: If the patron is known not to have control of this behavior, have another staff member help the patron. Often, lewd behavior will cease if the patron is being served by someone of the same gender.

PROBLEM: A patron becomes angry or frustrated when working with a certain staff member.
SOLUTION: So long as the patron is not abusive or violent, simply have another staff member help the patron. If the patron is violent or abusive, treat the situation as you would if the person did not have a disability.

PROBLEM: Inappropriate behavior persists despite the staff member involved and over a period of time.
SOLUTION: Library managers should become involved to determine the extent of the problem and negotiate a solution, if possible, with the patron.

PROBLEM: Staff members are reluctant to serve people with substance abuse problems or certain mental or emotional disorders.
SOLUTION: Library managers must implement and stand behind a policy which ensures that staff members will be supported if a patron becomes obscene or threatening.

PROBLEM: A patron is outwardly threatening or has a weapon.
SOLUTION: Call security immediately. The possibility of a disability causing the behavior should not be a factor where the safety of other patrons and staff members is in question.

COMMUNITY DATABASES AND OTHER INFORMATION SOURCES

There are a number of good resources for finding organizations that offer information and support to and about people with disabilities. You already have several good tools and procedures within your library, and you can easily use them to find resources for the community of people who are interested in disability information. Directories of national organizations will sometimes list state and local chapters. National associations and organizations are a rich resource of vertical file material, information about local chapters, and bibliographies for collection development. Don't forget the Internet. A number of good sites are listed later in this chapter.

Your local telephone book is a good starting place. It will help you locate community-based organizations and local chapters of national organizations. You may have to be creative and patient in using this source. The yellow pages listing of "Associations" may provide the most complete list. Looking up associations by type of disability can be cumbersome.

Many national organizations offer brochures and information sheets that will be valuable in learning the basics for communicating with people with disabilities.

National Easter Seal Society, 70 East Lake Street, Chicago, IL 60601, 312-726-6200 (voice), 312-726-4258 (TDD), 312-726-1494 (fax), "Awareness Is the First Step Toward Change: Tips for Disability Awareness."

Rochester Institute of Technology, National Technical Institute for the Deaf, Lyndon Baines Johnson Building, 52 Lomb Memorial Drive, Rochester, NY 14623-5604, 716-475-6834 (voice), 716-475-6205 (TDD), "Tips for Communicating with Deaf Employees," "Let's Communicate," (Basic Signs and Tips for Communicating with Deaf People).

American Foundation for the Blind, 15 West 16th Street, New York, NY 10011, "A Different Way of Seeing" (An open letter to children about people who are visually handicapped), "What Do You Do When You See a Blind Person?"

National Alliance for the Mentally Ill (NAMI), 2101 Wilson Boulevard, Suite 302, Arlington, VA 22201, 703-524-7600, NAMI helpline (for nearest chapter): 1-800-950-NAMI, "Outreach to Public Libraries" (1993), "Facts About Mental Illness."

The Arc: A National Organization on Mental Retardation, 500 E. Border Street, Suite 300, Arlington, TX 76010, 817-261-6003, "The Americans with Disabilities Act of 1990," "Access ADA: Free Assistance to Help Your Business Comply with Title II of the Americans with Disabilities Act," "Introduction to Mental Retardation," "Facts about Alcohol Use During Pregnancy"

Working with local organizations and activities can provide a great deal of local information that is otherwise difficult to attain. Attending community health fairs or meetings sponsored by hospitals and health organizations will produce armloads of brochures and contact information.

National organizations can also be helpful. You probably already have access to a number of library resources that will get you started finding general resources. For instance, try:

The Encyclopedia of Associations. (Frederick S. Ruffner and Margaret Fisk. Detroit, MI: Gale Research Co. Annual.) This standby provides a listing and directory of organizations in the United States, organized in a classified arrangement. It includes an alphabetical as well as geographic and executive indexes.

Ulrich's International Periodicals Directory. (New York: Bowker. Annual.) A comprehensive listing of periodicals, Ulrich's can point to magazines and journals of interest to people with disabilities, families, friends, and caregivers. As many of these are produced by organizations and associations, the publisher information can be a valuable component for follow-up inquiries.

The Complete Directory for People with Disabilities: Products, Resources, Books, Services. (Lakeville, CT: Grey House Pub. Annual.) Billed as "a one-stop sourcebook for individuals and professionals," this work contains directory information for providers of a wide variety of resources and services.

Disabilities, Children, and Libraries: Mainstreaming Services in Public Libraries and School Library Media Centers. (Linda Lucas Walling and Marilyn H. Karrenbrock. Englewood, CO: Libraries Unlimited, Inc., 1993.) Walling and Karrenbrock's chapter "Sources of Materials, Equipment, and Technology" provides directory information, program descriptions, and background on national organizations. Divided into sections of "sources serving children who are blind or physically disabled," "sources serving children who are deaf or hard of hearing," "sources for manipulative and adaptive materials and equipment," "sources for technology, organizations, agencies, and hotlines," and "other sources," this chapter provides extensive, usable directory information for adults as well as children.

Gallaudet University, National Information Center on Deafness. (800 Florida Ave. NE, Washington, DC 20002-3695.) The NICD produces the *Directory of National Organizations of and for Deaf and Hard of Hearing People.* "The directory was developed with information provided by each organization. All of the organizations are national and nonprofit and provide information on deaf and hard of hearing people and/or specific professional or consumer areas of interest." Also included is a list of state commissions/offices on deafness.

HEATH Resource Center. National Clearinghouse on Postsecondary Education for Individuals with Disabilities. (A Program of the American Council on Education. One Dupont Circle, Suite 800, Washington, DC 20036-1193.) *The HEATH Resource Directory* is a biennial "selection of resources in the major areas of interest in the field of postsecondary education and disability," including "advocacy, access, and awareness," "community integration," disability-specific organizations," "funding," "legal assistance," and "technology." Single copies are provided free by request, as are resource papers on many of the directory topics.

National Library Service for the Blind and Physically Handicapped. Library of Congress. (Library of Congress, Washington, DC 20542.) In addition to providing direct lending service to people who are blind, visually impaired, or physically handicapped, the NLS produces circulars, bibliographies, and directories listing agencies, services, and information resources.

Many libraries keep community information databases or files as an aid to patrons. These organizations can be a lifesaver to patrons who would otherwise feel isolated in the community. A community database may be kept on a sophisticated electronic database, or may simply be kept in files or on 3" x 5" cards. Whatever format is being used, community databases should contain the same elements.

- Both the acronym (if appropriate) and full name of the organization
- Full names and titles of organization contacts
- Address and phone information, including e-mail address, fax number, and TDD number, if applicable
- Membership requirements or restrictions and dues information
- Regular meeting information, including both time and place of meetings
- A short statement about the group's mission and objectives

Staff members responsible for gathering and updating information on community organizations will get more first-hand knowledge of the organizations and be more aware of the options available to patrons. They should, however, provide referrals to groups without judgment as they would when referring patrons to any other community service organization.

THE POWER OF THE INTERNET

Public Internet Access

Electronic access, like telephone access, can be an incredible boon to patrons with disabilities. Providing the opportunity to share insights and information with other people in similar situations from around the globe, Internet gateways can literally open a world of information to patrons. In recognition of the importance of this tool, many libraries are offering public Internet connection capabilities.

Extending these services to patrons with disabilities is, for the most part, the responsibility of library managers, who must ensure that interfaces are accessible even to patrons with visual or mobility impairments. Staff members, however, can help patrons best take advantage of the Internet connection.

Every staff member who works with the public must know how to use adaptive equipment and interfaces. All staff members should be encouraged to practice using alternative interfaces when they are using the computer so that they understand how the interfaces work under real-world conditions. Even in larger libraries where adaptive equipment is housed separately from the main computer area, staff members should know how the adaptive equipment works. This way, if a patron with a disability comes in when the adaptive equipment is broken, in use, or otherwise

---

DIAL-IN COMPUTER ACCESS: A BOON . . . AND A BUST

Dial-in computer access can be a real boon for patrons with disabilities. It allows them to use the patron catalog and other computerized services from their own homes and using their own familiar adaptive interfaces.

But dial-in access is only a benefit to those patrons who are fortunate or wealthy enough to own their own adaptive computer equipment. In special libraries where users have adaptive equipment in their offices, dial-in access may be sufficient to provide equal access to computer services. But in public, school, and academic libraries, dial-in access is not enough. Adaptive equipment must be available at the library itself to all constituents regardless of whether or not they can afford to purchase their own computer equipment.

---

not available, the staff member will know exactly what assistance the machine provides and will be better able to come up with alternative methods for getting the patron needed access.

Internet Reference Services

Even in libraries that do not offer public Internet access, the information network can be used to improve service to patrons with disabilities. Patrons with disabilities will have the same types of information needs as other patrons and will benefit in similar ways by being able to have library staff members expand the search for information and materials. The benefit of Internet searching can have a special immediate benefit for some people whose libraries do not have information about certain disabilities on hand. This is especially true in remote areas which may not have community groups to which patrons can be referred.

Through the Internet, libraries in all areas have access to numerous gophers, listservs, and web sites devoted to issues which concern people with disabilities. Library staff members can ask questions on behalf of patrons and receive answers, often in a matter of hours. Informational requests may be answered by a simple gopher or web site search in minutes.

Because the Internet can be such a powerful tool, everyone should learn to use it. By combining on-line and Internet access with our traditional reference and readers' advisory tools, we can provide excellent service in many formats to almost every patron.

A BASIC INTERNET GLOSSARY

This basic glossary is intended only to provide an introduction to terms used in this chapter. People who would like more information on using the Internet are referred to Allen C. Benson's *The Complete Internet Companion for Librarians* (New York: Neal-Schuman, 1994).

e-mail—electronic mail. Most people with Internet accounts have e-mail addresses which allow other people with Internet accounts to send them mail. Not all types of accounts allow for e-mail sending, and incompatible systems may be unable to exchange mail reliably.

ftp—file transfer protocol. A program which allows files to be transferred across the Internet. The term is also often used as a verb because "ftp" is entered as a command when logging on to a site which supports this type of file transfer.

gopher—an interface which uses a text menu from which the user chooses selections to get to different files, etc.

Internet—a loose network of computer links which allows worldwide communication among computers which have network access.

listserv—a mailing program which allows people interested in similar topics to exchange information. When a person joins a listserv, they receive all the mail which is sent to that topical group, even if it is not specifically addressed to them. People who belong to the listserv may also post mail to the list, contributing opinions and asking or answering questions. Several listservs devoted to issues of disability are included in the "ADA Internet Resources" list in this chapter.

post—to send mail to a public listserv. If you have a question on a particular subject, one good way to elicit responses is to post your request on an appropriate listserv. All people who subscribe to the listserv will receive your message.

site—an Internet host. Sites are often identified by the type of interface they use; thus, a web site is a host which uses a web interface (see below).

-space—a term appended to other Internet-related words which loosely implies the extent of that concept. Thus, gopherspace consists of all the information and services available by using Internet gophers. Similarly, cyberspace implies all the information and services available by using any networked interface.

usenet—similar to a listserv, but works a little more like a bulletin board. People can post or read messages whenever they like, and mail is not sent to their individual accounts.

web—(also known as world wide web or WWW) an interface similar to a gopher but using a multimedia graphical interface with both sound and images. Programs such as Lynx allow web sites to be negotiated by people with computers which do not support multimedia applications and by people with disabilities whose adaptive equipment is better able to use a textual interface.

ADA INTERNET RESOURCES

Listservs, gophers, and web sites can be very volatile, and this resource list includes only the ones which are targeted to libraries and general ADA information. These sites were active at the addresses listed as of September 1995. Explore them to find more resources which may be useful to you, your co-workers, and your patrons.

LISTSERVS

ADA-LAW@VM1.NODAK.EDU

subscriptions to: listserv@vm1.nodak.edu; **message**: sub ada-law yourfirstname yourlastname

A very general discussion list on ADA issues and advocacy.

ADANET@IUBVM.UCS.INDIANA.EDU

subscriptions to: listserv@iubvm.ucs.indiana.edu; **message**: sub adanet yourfirstname yourlastname

Discussion list for academic ADA coordinators, will also accept subscriptions from ADA coordinators at other institutions (like libraries) with similar goals.

ADAPT-L@AMERICAN.EDU

subscriptions to: listserv@american.edu; **message**: sub adapt-l yourfirstname yourlastname

General discussion list on all types of library adaptive technology.

AXSLIB@SJUVM.STJOHNS.EDU

subscriptions to: listserv@sjuvm.stjohns.edu; **message**: sub axslib-l yourfirstname yourlastname

Library access discussion list sponsored by EASI: Equal Access to Software and Information, an affiliate of the American Association for Higher Education.

GOPHERS

CORNUCOPIA OF DISABILITY INFORMATION

To get there: gopher val-dor.cc.buffalo.edu

Well-developed gopher of disability-related resources, also links to other systems.

EASI GOPHER

To get there: gopher sjuvm.stjohns.edu; select "disabilities" and then pick "EASI"

Includes CSUN (California State University Northridge) Center on Disabilities information. Other disabilities menus are available at the St. John's site as well.

GENERAL ADA INFORMATION

To get there: gopher handicap.shel.isc-br.com

Includes text of ADA and legal files as well as general ADA information.

INFORM GOPHER

To get there: gopher gopher.inform.umd.edu

Nicely laid-out gopher of disability sites and information.

ADA INTERNET RESOURCES (cont'd)

TRACE CENTER GOPHER

To get there: gopher trace.wisc.edu

Also sponsors a web site: http://trace.waisman.wisc.edu

One of the most useful sources of adaptive technology answers to access problems. Includes some free programs which may help improve computer access, including AccessDOS and Access Pack for Windows.

TELNET SITE

ENABLE.WVNET.EDU

To get there: telnet enable.wvnet.edu. If this doesn't work, try sending a message to enable@rtcz. icdi.wvu.edu

Includes many discussion lists, accommodation ideas, and the full text of the ADA.

WEB SITES

DISABILITY MALL

address: http://disability.com

Publishes a "tip of the month" and offers products for people with disabilities which can be ordered on-screen.

KNOWLEDGE INDUSTRIES WEB SITE

address: http://www.pavilion.co.uk/CommonRoom/DisabilitiesAccess/

Includes a lot of interesting information, plus full articles on aspects of computer access by people with disabilities.

RIT WEB SITE

address: http://ultb.isc.rit.edu/~nrcgsh

Web site offering a broad range of disability-related information.

SCIENCE/ENGINEERING/MATH SITE

address: http://www.rit.edu/~easi/easisem.html

Specifically dedicated to providing access information for engineering, science, and math professionals.

RESOURCES

Jahoda, Gerald. *How Do I Do This When I Can't See What I'm Doing? Information Processing for the Visually Disabled.* Washington, DC: National Library Service for the Blind and Physically Handicapped, The Library of Congress, 1993.

This is an absolute "must have" for all library collections. Written in a clear and concise style by a library and information science educator who is himself visually impaired, this work focuses on ABILITY. For the patron who is visually impaired, this wise little book offers advice on everyday living skills, computers as assistive devices, personal information management systems, job hunting, leisure activities, techniques for independent living, and support groups. For those who will be offering services to people who are visually impaired, Jahoda gives insight into the needs and abilities of individuals, provides important information (such as the factors that have a bearing on selection of reading method) and gives precise instructions to service providers, for instance, "instructions for readers who record for us."

Karp, Rashelle S. *Library Services for Disabled Individuals.* Boston: G.K. Hall & Co., 1991.

Karp's book is notable for its attention to individuals with learning disabilities (chapter by Karp) and individuals who are mentally retarded (chapter by Pamela Gent), two groups often overlooked in discussions of library services to people with disabilities. Also included are chapters on services to individuals who are print-handicapped (Beth Perry) or who are hearing impaired or deaf (Phyllis I. Dalton). All chapters are straightforward and clearly written, giving definitions, characteristics of the respective user groups, pertinent legislation, user needs, and lists of major agencies and organizations. Karp also offers hard-to-find sensitizing activities for staff training.

Norton, Melanie J., and Gail L. Kovalik, editors. *Libraries Serving an Underserved Population: Deaf and Hearing-Impaired Patrons. Library Trends* 41 (Summer 1992).

Norton and Kovalik have assembled a fine group of essays covering a variety of topics related to service provision for deaf and hearing-impaired patrons. In addition to an excellent overview of library services, guidelines for communication techniques, collection development and information retrieval on deafness, bibliographic instruction services, and captioned films are included. Bibliographies of fiction featuring deaf characters and resources of the New York State Library provide useful information. A discussion of standards for library media centers in schools for the deaf and the inclusion of the New York Library Association's "Guidelines for Libraries Serving Persons with a Hearing Impairment" serve as models for policy development.

Ross, Catherine Sheldrick and Patricia Dewdney. *Communicating Professionally: A How-To-Do-It Manual for Library Applications.* How-To-Do-It Manuals for Libraries Series No. 3. New York: Neal-Schuman Publishers, Inc., 1989.

Ross and Dewdney provide excellent tips for communicating one on one or in groups. Although this manual is written to improve communication skills with all patrons, it is very useful in providing techniques to assure effective communication with patrons with disabilities.

Saricks, Joyce G. and Nancy Brown. *Readers' Advisory Service in the Public Library*. Chicago: American Library Association, 1989.

Saricks and Brown provide a good introduction to readers' advisory services. While they do not specifically talk about services to special clientele groups, the basics of readers' advisory services to all patrons serve as the foundation for appropriate services to people with disabilities.

Systems and Procedures Exchange Center. *Library Services for Persons with Disabilities*. SPEC Kit 176. Washington, DC: Association of Research Libraries, 1991.

This SPEC Kit provides copies of procedures for use of the TTD/TTY as well as etiquette sheets and tips on communicating with people with disabilities.

3 CIRCULATING MATERIALS IN THE LIBRARY

One of the main functions of most libraries is to circulate materials. Establishing circulation policies and procedures which provide equal access to patrons with disabilities may involve some creativity. By setting reasonable application policies, you help ensure that patrons with disabilities do not have to jump through hoops to get library cards. By making the circulation area accessible and inviting, you increase the likelihood that the experience will be enjoyable for all parties. And by anticipating contingencies and giving employees the authority to be flexible enough to meet them, you foster an attitude of service excellence.

Each person, individually, can improve service levels by emphasizing goals, rather than procedures. If, for example, a driver's license is required to get an adult card, you can allow a patron who does not drive to present alternative means of proving identification. If the physical check-out area is designed with an imposingly high service counter, you can devise ways to serve patrons who cannot reach the counter. To be effective, these accommodations must be made in a way that is not condescending or patronizing to the patron, and that emphasizes the importance of service.

THE PHYSICAL ENVIRONMENT

Under the Americans with Disabilities Act, library circulation desks, both check-in and check-out, must have at least one area 36" long and not more than 36" high. Unfortunately, some libraries have not yet remodeled their counters. Others have the extensions, but do not keep them clear, using them instead as holding areas for materials going to and from the desk. Following some easy reminders will help keep the circulation area accessible and improve communications for all.

- Where desk extensions or cut-outs exist, make sure they are kept clear. Keep a flat book truck on hand if temporary storage space is needed; this has the added advantage of portability, eliminating the need to lift and carry materials.
- If a terminal is installed at the accessible counter section, station a staff member there, rather than having all staff members stand behind the taller counter sections.

- If the accessible area is not always staffed, keep an eye out for patrons who use wheelchairs or are of short stature and automatically move to the accessible counter before patrons have to ask.
- Keep a supply of soft lead pencils and reasonably sized scrap paper accessible to the patrons. If theft is a problem, it is better to tie the pencil down than to make patrons ask for one.
- Keep a hand magnifier at the desk for patrons to use when completing applications, etc.
- Arrange lighting so that staff members' faces are not in a shadow.
- Do not eat or chew gum at the desk.
- If a TDD is available in the department, ensure that all staff members who may answer the phone or help the public know how to use it.

CHECKING BOOKS IN AND OUT

Once the physical environment has been made inviting and an accessible counter space added, checking books in and out for patrons with disabilities should proceed as for any other patrons. When there is not an extension to the desk, circulation desk employees should ask patrons whether they need assistance getting their books on and off the counter. As noted before, it is the patron who is best able to judge whether or not help is needed. When patrons say no, that should be accepted, no matter how difficult the procedure looks to the employee.

The importance of patience cannot be overly stressed. It may take some people longer than others to open their books or find their library cards. Staff members should remain pleasant and should continue to focus on the patron being served. "Sympathetic" glances to other patrons in line are rude and inappropriate; it is also rude to start working on the next patron's books before finishing with the patron being helped.

When checking out or renewing books, a few courtesies can help ensure that patrons understand the terms of circulation.

- Orally announce the due date and point it out on the card or slip.
- If other clues (different colored cards, etc.) are used to distinguish books which have different return dates or conditions, point these out as well. Alternatively, post an example of each type of card or stamp with a clear explanation of its meaning.

Sometimes, patrons will ask for reference help at the circulation desk. Except in extreme circumstances, patrons should be politely referred to the appropriate department, even if other patrons are not waiting. Otherwise, patrons may begin using the circulation desk for reference help as a matter of course, leading to frustration when busy circulation staff members cannot handle patron requests or when they simply do not have the tools at hand to answer questions.

Some types of cognitive and mental disabilities interfere with date memories. When patrons mention that they have trouble with dates, cross out old due dates and circle or highlight the correct one.

- If reserve books are checked out on an hourly basis and the time due written in by hand, be sure to write legibly in dark ink.
- If due dates are noted on stickers, make sure that old stickers are promptly removed when books are returned.

A Special Note on Circulation Receipts

Some libraries give patrons receipts and do not mark due dates on the books. This may be fine for most patrons, but for some people it is more effective to have each book labeled with its due date. Receipts may be more difficult to read than a bold black stamp, especially if the printer ribbon is wearing out. Receipts are also more easily misplaced or inadvertently destroyed than pocket cards, which is especially frustrating to patrons with disabilities affecting memory. When books are pocketed or have due date slips affixed to them, ask patrons whether they would like date due cards, stamps, or stickers in addition to their receipts.

Extended Borrowing Privileges

Some libraries offer special cards with extended borrowing privileges to senior citizens. If this special status is offered, it is reasonable to extend it to patrons with disabilities as well. Some people with mobility impairments have a hard time obtaining regular and reliable transportation to the library. Additionally, some people with cognitive disabilities may need to check out a book for a longer period of time to thoroughly read and understand it. Allowing these patrons to check out books for extended periods offers several benefits, especially in public libraries.

If your library does not have books either pocketed or slipped, you can purchase inexpensive removable labels which can be stamped with the due date and affixed to book and magazine covers, etc., without harming the material. Be sure to get removable labels, and consider using an unusual color so that the labels are easy to spot and to distinguish from their more permanent peers.

- Patrons with cognitive or communications difficulties which make using telephone renewal services difficult will have to use those services less often.
- Patrons will be able to check out best-sellers and popular books which cannot be renewed without worrying about having to rush to finish them.
- Patrons who rely on family members for transportation to get and return books will have a little more time to coordinate schedules.

ANTICIPATING CIRCULATION CHALLENGES

The key to service excellence lies in flexibility. Staff members must be ready to solve circulation problems with minimal fuss and

---

Figure 3.1   AUTHORIZATION TO CHECK OUT MATERIALS ON PATRON'S BEHALF

This form must be signed in the presence of a library staff member. If it is not possible for the patron to come to the library for this purpose, the form should be notarized before being returned by the patron's authorized agent.

PATRON'S NAME:_____

PATRON'S LIBRARY CARD NUMBER:_____

PATRON'S ADDRESS:_____

_____

PATRON'S TELEPHONE NUMBER:_____

I hereby authorize the person(s) listed below to check out library books on my behalf using the card number above. I understand that I am responsible for all books checked out to my library card by my authorized agent(s). I further understand that this authority is not transferrable, and only the person(s) named below will be able to check out books on my behalf.

Name(s) of person(s) authorized to check out books on behalf of the patron named above:

_____

_____

_____

PATRON'S SIGNATURE:_____   DATE:_____

should be given some authority to do so. Typical problems associated with circulation can be anticipated and prevented with minimal planning.

PROBLEM: Patrons with temporary disabilities wish to take advantage of extended check-out periods.
SOLUTION: Have at least one person at the circulation desk authorized to override the due date on a one-time basis.
SOLUTION: For patrons with disabilities which will last more than a few weeks, update the patron records and change the status to allow the longer check-out period. Find out for how long the patrons will be affected by these temporary disabilities, and set cards to expire at the end of the temporary period. Place notes in the comments field instructing staff members to reset patron cards to the normal check-out status once the period expires.

PROBLEM: Patrons with disabilities have attendants come to the library to retrieve the books they want.
SOLUTION: Have patrons complete a permission slip authorizing their aides to check out books on their behalf (page 54). Either have the aide present this slip at each check-out or keep the slip on file and add a note to the patron's record authorizing the aide to check out materials.
SOLUTION: Call the patron to verify that the aide has permission to check out books.
SOLUTION: Encourage patrons to call in advance. This is especially useful if staff members are usually the ones who select materials for these patrons, because the books will be waiting when the aides arrive.

Renewals

In general, patrons with disabilities should follow the same rules on renewals as other patrons. Overall borrowing time limits, number of renewals, and renewal policies for books on waiting lists should be uniformly applied. Staff members should have the authority to be somewhat flexible, however, when interpreting rules, especially for patrons who find it difficult to visit the library. Library managers should consider allowing telephone renewals or renewals by caretakers for these patrons. In many cases, it is also appropriate to give staff members the authority to grant one- to three-day extensions on books that cannot be renewed to allow patrons a couple of extra days to get books back without incurring a fine.

Fines

Again, as a rule, people with disabilities should be charged the same fines as people who do not have disabilities. If the library routinely waives fines for patrons returning books late because of personal emergencies, the same procedure should be followed when an emergency affects someone because they have a disability. A transit strike which affects non-emergency transport of people with disabilities might be one such instance. The important point to remember is that the disability in and of itself is not an emergency, and it is patronizing to treat it as such by routinely waiving fines for people with disabilities.

PLACING HOLDS

If you are responsible for placing holds on items (especially over the phone), remember to let patrons know about any alternative formats that are available. This ensures that patrons will reserve the material in the most accessible format possible. Patrons may not be aware that large print or audio versions of a new book are available. On the other hand, they may think the library has a large print or audio version of material when, in fact, the library does not. Always ask patrons for format preference up front and let them know whether that format is available.

INTERLIBRARY LOAN

For the most part, interlibrary loan procedures should be the same for patrons with disabilities as for those without. There are, however, a few exceptions.

- Libraries which do not normally exchange books or certain types of books (such as reference materials) among outlets should do so if the outlet at which the material is held is not accessible.
- Telephone renewal privileges may be granted to patrons with disabilities who have transportation problems even if they are not regularly granted to other patrons.
- If the library is obtaining a book through interlibrary loan because, although it has the material, it is not owned in an accessible format, the library may choose to waive any associated fee which might normally be charged.

Savvy patrons who are requesting popular materials may ask how long the hold lists are for both large and small print, planning to place their holds on the shorter lists. Even if library policy allows patrons to do this, library staff members should emphasize that alternative formats are purchased specifically as an aid to people who could not enjoy the book in standard print.

Accepting Materials Borrowed through the NLS or a State Library

Many people with visual or motor impairments which do not allow them to use printed books borrow Braille and taped materials through a state library or the National Library Service for the Blind and Physically Handicapped. Unless your library has an arrangement with these institutions, it is important not to accept returns from these libraries. Materials returned to the wrong library can sometimes sit for days until they are packaged to send where they belong. By being "nice" to the patron, the library is in fact keeping the material out of circulation. The library may also risk being held responsible for material over which it exercises no control.

APPLICATIONS FOR LIBRARY CARDS

Having a library card is like holding a key to information. Most libraries require that card-holders belong to a specific group—they must either live or work within the library's jurisdiction, go to school at the library's institution, or work at the library's company. Library staff members must ensure that people who receive library cards meet the qualifications to be a cardholder, but they must also ensure that their procedures are flexible enough so that people who are otherwise qualified to have library cards are not denied the opportunity because of their disabilities.

Libraries which serve large numbers of people with disabilities should provide applications in alternative formats. Some possibilities are:

- Braille applications which can also be completed in Braille (be sure somebody on your staff can read Braille before you do this);
- applications which can be completed using a computer screen and then printed out for signature (this allows patrons to use adaptive interfaces to complete their own applications); and
- large print applications.

Staff members of libraries which do not have applications in alternative formats should be ready to help people who have difficulty with the standard application complete the form, or be willing to complete most of the form (except the signature) from the patron's dictation.

Examples of identification and proofs of address which may be accepted, so long as they have both the patron's name and address printed on them:

- Voter registration card
- Rent receipt or lease
- Payroll check or stub
- Workplace ID
- School ID
- Utility or cable bill
- Health insurance card
- Bank-issued checks
- Letter from administrator of halfway house or shelter

Anticipating Common Problems

Whether or not the library has application forms in alternative formats, problems may arise when patrons with disabilities apply for cards. Combined patience, flexibility, and preparation will ensure that staff members overcome these problems and that patrons will not be unfairly denied the opportunity to get their own library cards.

PROBLEM: A patron cannot complete the application because of a print disability which makes it difficult or impossible for the patron to read the form.
SOLUTION: Keep a hand magnifier at the desk and allow the patron to use it when completing the form.
SOLUTION: If the library has a CCD magnifier, allow the patron to take the application to the department with the magnifier, complete the form there, then return the completed form to the circulation desk.
SOLUTION: Read each form entry to the patron and indicate where the answer goes.
SOLUTION: Offer to complete the form from the patron's dictation.

PROBLEM: Patron cannot complete the application because of a physical disability making it difficult or impossible for the patron to write.
SOLUTION: Complete the form for the patron. Make sure, however, that all patrons sign their own applications and cards. Blind and severely visually impaired people usually carry a signature guide or can use a rule so that this is not a problem. A patron with extremely limited motor control has likely encountered this situation numerous times. Indicate that the patron needs to sign at a certain spot and then wait for directions from the patron.

PROBLEM: The patron does not have a driver's license, sheriff's ID, or passport for identification or address verification.
SOLUTION: Library managers should develop a list of acceptable alternative proof of identification. Be sure patrons do not have any of the accepted materials before denying them cards.
SOLUTION: Give patrons a printed form listing the types of ID or proof of address which may be used by library applicants. Be sure the phone number of the circulation department is included on the form in case patrons have questions later on.

PROBLEM: An adult without majority status wants to apply for a card, but her legal guardian is not with her. An aide or attendant volunteers to sign for the patron.

SOLUTION: Secure the signature of the patron's legal guardian before issuing a card. Because it is the guardian who will be fiscally responsible for any material checked out on the card, the guardian must be present when the application is presented and the card issued. Unless the aide is also the legal guardian, do not allow the aide to sign for the card.

PROBLEM: A guardian or parent cannot come to the library to sign for their child's or ward's card because of a disability.
SOLUTION: Allow the applicant to take the application home. The parent or guardian may sign and have the signature notarized. The applicant may then return the completed, notarized form to the library.

A library card can be a friend for life. It is also often the one "status" symbol which is available to all. When you make your circulation policies inclusive and develop meaningful strategies to serve everyone, you help ensure that all people, regardless of disability, will carry their library cards with pride and use them often.

RESOURCES

Walling, Linda Lucas, and Marilyn H. Karrenbrock. *Disabilities, Children, and Libraries: Mainstreaming Services in Public Libraries and School Library Media Centers*. Englewood, CO: Libraries Unlimited, Inc., 1993.
    Walling and Karrenbrock discuss the importance (and ease) of adapting circulation and reserve policies and procedures for youth with disabilities and note the administrative and political value of keeping statistics. Many of their ideas can be adapted for use with any patron. This is the only book we found which gives serious attention to materials circulation to patrons with disabilities.

4 OUTREACH SERVICES

The passage of the Americans with Disabilities Act (ADA) and the increase in the percentage of people in our country who are senior citizens have led to an increased demand for library outreach services. Outreach services may range from books-by-mail to small weekly "library hours" at nursing homes to elaborately stocked bookmobiles. Outreach services should provide maximal library services even in a minimal setting, and their importance to patrons, especially to those who otherwise would have no access to the library, cannot be overestimated. We must bear in mind constantly the importance of library services to the people served by outreach. Our programs must be designed not with a "pack 'em up and go" attitude, but with the same care and consideration we use when serving patrons within library walls.

PRELIMINARY CONSIDERATIONS

Library managers must thoroughly prepare the groundwork if outreach services are to proceed smoothly. Be sure the following matters are settled before any staff outreach is begun.

- Obtain proper insurance or vehicle licenses. If the library's policy will not cover insurance for people who use their own vehicles for library business, be sure that a library vehicle is available for outreach or that the library's mileage reimbursement takes into account the higher insurance rates these staff members will have.
- If staff members or volunteers will make deliveries of more than a few bags of books, be sure a library car is available for their use; the wear and tear of acting as a delivery van rapidly takes its toll on a regular passenger vehicle.
- Negotiate arrangements with institutions. Visit the site to ensure the facilities will accommodate an outreach program. Address issues of patron access to information, any circulation policies or restrictions, etc. at this time.
- Prepare a preliminary site visit sheet for each site which will be served (page 61). Modify the sample site visit sheets as necessary to reflect local considerations.

Overall Start-Up and Maintenance Ideas for an Excellent Program

No matter what form outreach takes, there are certain guidelines which must be followed to ensure consistent, excellent service.

Suggested places to advertise outreach services:

• Press in all media—radio, television, newspapers, and local magazines

• Displays on buses, subway cars, etc., and public kiosks

• Local computer bulletin boards

• Local offices of disabilities advocacy organizations

• Local offices of organizations which serve people with disabilities

• Local council on aging or similar agency office

• Social welfare agencies

• Schools, including those serving deaf or visually impaired students

• Nursing homes and retirement communities

• Doctors' offices

• Ideally, outreach should be performed by professional staff members. When this is not possible, professional staff members should visit each site on a rotating basis to emphasize the library's commitment to service.

• When paraprofessionals or volunteers will perform outreach services, they must receive proper training and monitoring/supervision.

• Even when professional staff members are performing outreach, they cannot provide the full range of services available in the library. Brochures covering remote access opportunities, such as telephone reference services, local library television programming and the like should be brought along on visits to remind patrons that they do have access to other services.

• All staff members performing or administering outreach programs must read and understand any library policies related to these services.

• The outreach coordinator or librarian and outreach staff members must meet regularly to review any problems or strengths of the collection. Front-line staff are likely to be more familiar with patron needs regarding both material content and format, and should have input into collection decisions.

• Outreach staff members must remain aware of the library's full range of services and the context within which their services are being offered. This is especially important when outreach duties occupy all an employee's time, as that person can easily become isolated from the rest of the library.

• Outreach staff members must keep their schedules. Scheduling problems need to be worked out as far in advance as possible, to give patrons ample notice. Any changes or interruptions in service should be thoroughly advertised through those media which the affected patrons are likely to see.

OUTREACH TO INSTITUTIONS

Even libraries which offer no individual book delivery and which have no bookmobiles often provide library services at nursing homes and other institutions. Although each type of institution has a different profile, many present similar challenges to staff members.

Figure 4.1   SITE VISITATION SHEET FOR OUTREACH TO INSTITUTIONS, RETIREMENT CENTERS, ETC.

Facility name:_____

Location:_____

Parking arrangements:_____

Where is the meeting with patrons held?_____

What are the scheduled days and times?_____

Who is the institution's contact person?

    Name:_____   Phone:_____

How many residents or patients live at the facility?_____

Will the residents (check all that apply)

_____   browse for books at a common location?

_____   need to have books brought to individual rooms?

_____   have books dropped off for specific patrons?

_____   have books and other materials left for an in-house library?

What format(s) will be needed by residents (check all that apply)?

_____   Regular print hardcover

_____   Regular print paperback

_____   Large print

_____   Magazines

_____   Audiotapes

_____   Videotapes

_____   Other formats such as multimedia packages:

Additional comments:

Institutional Etiquette

As mentioned above, library management should have worked out the arrangement to provide outreach services before the first staff member visits. Staff members can build on this foundation by following a few basic etiquette tips.

- If the unloading zone is separate from the parking area, unload quickly and leave unloaded books out of the flow of traffic into the building.
- Park in the library's designated area. If no space is available in that area and you must park someplace else, let the receptionist know. If you are blocking someone's space, ask the receptionist where you can park, and move the car there.
- Always greet the receptionist or front desk employee and identify yourself.
- Follow the institution's security measures, even if they seem inconvenient.
- If you are issued a visitor's badge, wear it.
- Ask front desk staff members about patrons who have been absent or who are known to be in the hospital, etc. Be sure to keep your comments positive and professional.
- If something is not right, ask the front desk staff members for help, but remember that they are not the ones who caused the problem and, many times, they may not be authorized to solve it, either.
- Do not ask institution employees to help load and unload books, unless this service was part of the agreement made when the library arranged to visit the site.
- If a patron falls or is otherwise injured, summon help from institution employees, who are trained to deal with this type of emergency. Do not attempt to aid the patron yourself; you may make things worse.

Following these rules will smooth institution personnel contact enormously. Staff members who are treated well by library visitors can become very helpful advocates of library service, and outreach workers can consider themselves, in some sense, to be ambassadors to this community.

Outreach staff members should use the same courtesy when dealing with patrons that is expected of staff within the library.

- Always introduce yourself and make it a point to repeat the patron's name. If you cannot remember who a patron is, apologize and ask the patron directly.

"I'm not your honey!"
"Honey" and "dear" are terms that should be reserved for your immediate family members. To call elderly people "honey," "dear," "sweetie" or the like is unprofessional. Worse yet, it is insulting to patrons, implying that they are not adults and can be treated like children. Even a patron who cannot clearly communicate may be able to hear you, so unless you are intimately related to a patron, you should avoid this presumptuous terminology.

Just because you find a book bloody or explicit does not mean that older patrons need to be protected from it. Many senior patrons do want "clean" books, and their wishes should be respected, but many a kind grandmother enjoys gory crime and racy sex. Remember to select books based on what patrons want, not on what you think is appropriate for "someone their age."

- Use the same rules for communication as you would at the library, being sure to speak clearly and in a regular tone of voice, and to speak directly to the patron, not to a nurse or aide.
- Keep the access route and display area clear of library bags, chairs, boxes, or other obstructions. Chairs used by patrons who are browsing should be kept to a minimum and placed close to the display table but out of the flow of traffic.
- Keep a list of patron requests and reading interests and bring books which are matched to these.
- If asked for a recommendation in a genre with which you are unfamiliar, be honest. Explain that you really cannot judge that work, but add any recommendations or evaluations you may have heard from other patrons at the institution.
- Remember that elderly patrons who read voraciously have usually done so throughout their lives. Although they may want to read or re-read classics, they often want new fiction. Finding a steady supply of large print books for patrons who can read 15 or 20 books in a week can be quite a challenge. Consequently, you must keep good records of reading history and interests, establish a rapport with patrons, and keep an eye out for new releases.

Books checked out during outreach should be charged out to the patron taking the book. This can be done by issuing each patron a library card and then entering the transactions into the library computer at a later time, or outreach staff members can charge books by manually using the patron's name and a book card. Some snags, however, are bound to crop up in any institutional outreach situation.

PROBLEM: Patrons lend books among themselves or to non-resident friends and relatives without going through the library staff members.
SOLUTION: Ask patrons to inform you if they have exchanged books with another person since your last visit.
SOLUTION: Remind patrons that books checked out for outreach are only intended for use by people who are residents of the institution and not to be lent to visitors.
SOLUTION: Remind patrons that they are responsible for the books they check out. If the book is late, address your concerns to the responsible patron, not the friend.

Figure 4.2 SURVEY OF PATRON READING INTERESTS

Name:_____   Date:_____

Please take a moment to complete this form and return it to me at my next visit.

In general, I like the following types of fiction (list the names of authors or specific types you especially enjoy):

_____	Adventure/Spy stories	_____	Classic-style British mysteries
_____	Animal stories	_____	Poetry
_____	Best-sellers	_____	Romance
_____	Classics	_____	Series romance (Harlequin, etc.)
_____	Family sagas	_____	Historical romance
_____	Fantasy and/or Science Fiction	_____	Regency romance
_____	General fiction/Literature	_____	Romantic suspense
_____	Horror and occult	_____	Short stories
_____	Humor	_____	Westerns
_____	Mysteries	_____	Other fiction:
		_____	I do not read fiction

In general, I like the following types of non-fiction (list any authors or subjects in which you are particularly interested):

_____	Philosophy/Religion	_____	Cooking and food
_____	Social concerns /Current events	_____	Arts, crafts, and/or collectibles
_____	Science, mathematics, and/or technology	_____	Games and sports
_____	Nature–animals (including pets and pet care)	_____	Essays
		_____	Regional history
_____	Nature–flowers and plants (including growing plants)	_____	American history
		_____	World history
_____	Aviation or nautical books	_____	Travel
_____	Home design and decorating	_____	Biographies
		_____	Other non-fiction:
		_____	I do not read non-fiction

Please list any authors or topics that are of particular interest to you:

Additional comments:

PROBLEM: Patrons are issued regular library cards but forget to bring them.
SOLUTION: Keep a list of names and card numbers and bring it with you.
SOLUTION: Write down the patron's name and look up the card number when you return to the library.

PROBLEM: A nurse or attendant is dispatched to pick up books for a patron.
SOLUTION: Allow them to do so. If library staff members pick out particular books in advance, check them out in advance as well, to save the nurse's or aide's time.

PROBLEM: A patron has requested a book, but does not come to pick it up.
SOLUTION: If possible, leave the book at the front desk or with the activities director and ask them to see that the patron gets it.
SOLUTION: Bring back the same selections at the next visit.

PROBLEM: Patrons have individual cards, and their records are purged after a book is returned. Library staff members picking out books for patrons cannot tell if the patrons have read the books before.
SOLUTION: Keep a book card to track who has already read which books.
SOLUTION: If a book card is impossible, keep a database of who has had what books. Remember that this information is confidential and should be used only for the purpose of selecting books to take to patrons.

PROBLEM: Patrons return books checked out at outreach to a "regular" library location.
SOLUTION: Use a distinctive date-due card or sticker. If different people keep track of different outreach sites, these should be coded to indicate from which outreach site they were borrowed. The book can then be routed to the person responsible for that site, who can check it in and replace the book card. Alert circulation staff members to this procedure.

PROBLEM: A few books are not returned.
SOLUTION: Check with front desk staff members to see if the books have been left there.
SOLUTION: Ask the activities director to publish a search request in the institution's newsletter.

SOLUTION: Ask the activities director to look in the institution's library.

SOLUTION: Write off the books as lost.

PROBLEM: One patron has a problem with outstanding items.

SOLUTION: Explain to the patron that you cannot allow more books to be checked out until the outstanding books have been returned.

SOLUTION: If the patron has left the facility, check to be sure the books were not returned to the front desk.

SOLUTION: If the patron has died, let the activities director know if any library books remain outstanding; the activities director can get notice to the next of kin.

SOLUTION: Write off the books as lost.

PROBLEM: The institution has many patrons who never return books.

SOLUTION: Give each patron an individual library card with the same terms and qualifications as with any other library card, and circulate books only to those patrons who have cards.

SOLUTION: Install a collection of unprocessed books at the location. While this is hardly optimal and should be done only as a last resort, it does allow the library to provide some type of service at the institution.

PROBLEM: Doctors, family members, institution administrators, or other people object to something which has been given to the patron.

SOLUTION: Explain that you must follow the library's policy regarding intellectual freedom and bring patrons the material they request. Take the name of the complainant, report the incident, and have library management respond.

SOLUTION: If the patron does not have majority status, allow the patron's legal guardian to select material for him/her. Explain, however, that if the patron attends library time unaccompanied by the legal guardian, access to material cannot be restricted. Refer the complainant to library administration if the parent or guardian needs further clarification of this policy.

PROBLEM: Patrons request new popular books which have long hold lists.

SOLUTION: Periodically review issues of magazines which review or announce upcoming releases and place holds for the institution on books which are sure to be popular among its clients.

SOLUTION: Reiterate to library circulation staff members the importance of reserving holds on large print materials for those patrons who actually need them.

Special Considerations at Hospitals

The most challenging aspects of outreach services to hospitals lie with management. All of the normal preliminary agreements must be formed, but hospitals may have a much more rigid hierarchy, may wish to restrict patron access to certain types of information, and may be far more sensitive to issues of liability than other types of institution. Any agreement worked out to provide outreach service must explicitly address these issues in advance if library service is to be successful.

Even with an excellent arrangement in place, hospitals present a real outreach challenge for staff members. Patients may have stays of a week or less. People from infancy to old age are represented. Family members are often much more visible than in long-term care institutions. Patient conditions are often volatile, and even long-term patients may have conditions which vary drastically from visit to visit. Patrons may be moved from one room to another, or to another part of the hospital entirely.

Even though the patrons may change more frequently, it is important for the same staff members to consistently visit the same institutions. Every institution has its own "feel," and good outreach staff members will learn to use the tone of the hospital as a tool to selecting the materials that are likely to be in the most demand at that location. Consistency can also help establish good relations with hospital management, a big help when trying to negotiate any changes in the nature or extent of services.

Special Considerations at Juvenile Facilities

Children's institutions serve children. This obvious fact leads to a special challenge when providing outreach services to these locations. It is easy to say that parents must accompany a child to the library to check out materials, but when that child is in an institution, a parent may not be available during library time. This means that if a child checks out materials deemed inappropriate by a counselor or parent, the staff members may be considered responsible for it. At the same time, a parent who did not authorize library services for a child may deny financial responsibility for materials checked out by the child but damaged or not returned. These are largely management problems, but they affect staff members serving institutionalized children who must be the ones to tell the children that their access to library materials is either restricted or cut off.

Staff members can be best supported by a policy similar to the one in place for hospital service. Access policies and intellectual freedom statements related to children's services should be re-

You must fight a double urge and not act in a condescending way to young patrons. The natural urge to protect and coddle children can be combined with sympathy for a child with a disability to create an atmosphere which is sickly and stifling. Remember that your focus should be on the young patrons, not their disabilities.

Figure 4.3   SAMPLE LIBRARY SERVICES AUTHORIZATION FORM FOR PARENTS

Library Services to Children

The Pleasantville Library visits institutions and other facilities on a regular basis. If you wish to allow your child to participate in our program, please read, complete, and sign the permission slip below and return it to your child's counsellor or to the Pleasantville Library children's department. Be sure to type or print legibly. If you have any questions about these services, please call our children's librarian at 555-5007.

To whom it may concern:

I hereby give permission for my child, _____ , to receive library services while a resident at _____. I understand that my child has the same access to library materials as with a normal children's library card, and that I am responsible for any books or materials checked out by my child.

Parent's signature:_____   Date:_____

Parent's name (please print or type):_____

Address:_____

Telephone number:_____

While dial-in access is becoming more widespread, especially in academic and large public libraries, it puts most of the burden of accessibility and accommodation on the patron, rather than the library. In addition, staff member contact is usually minimal and related only to providing computer help when it is needed. For these reasons, electronic access as a method of outreach to individuals with disabilities does not generally present any special challenge to front-line staff members and is not covered here.

printed and given to institution management with the request that they be forwarded on for signature by the parents. The signed statements can then be kept on file at the institution.

If library access must be restricted only to children who have regular library cards, a collection of unprocessed gift books and discarded duplicates should be provided for other children. Because the intellectual freedom issue will be important even for this "free" collection, library managers should be sure that institution staff members provide the statements of access to all patrons, not just those who have library cards. Only those children whose parents have agreed to allow their children to have library privileges should be allowed to come to the library time, although other programs such as storytelling or special presentations should be open to all.

OUTREACH TO INDIVIDUALS

Library outreach to individuals takes three forms: personal delivery of materials, sending items by mail, and electronic access from the patron's home. Special libraries usually provide individual services to their patrons as a matter of policy. School and academic libraries are usually able to coordinate services to students with disabilities through counselors and classroom teachers (some special considerations for school and academic librarians are given at the end of the chapter). But public libraries must determine the information needs of their communities, and then must develop and maintain their own programs to meet those needs. Often this is accomplished either through personal delivery of materials or through a books-by-mail program.

PERSONAL DELIVERY

Personal delivery carries with it a number of benefits and a host of potential liabilities. On the positive side, regular personal contact with a library staff member can provide a vital link to the outside world for a patron whose disabilities make it difficult to travel. Although many patrons with severe disabilities are quite active in the community, there are some who have few personal contacts outside of caregivers and family members. The opportunity to talk with someone who provides the patron with books and informational materials can make a real difference in these people's lives.

Before initiating any type of personal delivery, the library must have a policy detailing who will qualify for the service. Some type of confirmation that the patron is unable to travel to the library should also be required, in the same vein as any other request for special services to people with disabilities (page 70). Independent

---

**Figure 4.4 PLEASANTVILLE LIBRARY
APPLICATION FOR FREE AT-HOME LIBRARY SERVICE TO INDIVIDUALS**

Patrons who are home- or institution-bound may receive at-home delivery of books from the Pleasantville Library. If you are unable to read standard printed material because of a disability, you may be eligible to receive audiocassettes, Braille, or other format material from the National Library Service for the Blind and Physically Handicapped. Call the Pleasantville Library Reference Department at 555-5002 (voice) or 555-5006 (TDD) for more information.

Please complete the application below, have it signed by your doctor, and return it to any branch of the Pleasantville Library. All information on this application will be kept confidential.

Please Type or Print Neatly

First name:_____   Last name:_____

Street address (We cannot use a post office box number as your address):

_____

City:_____ State:_____ Zip Code:_____

Telephone Number:_____

You may arrange to have books mailed to your home, or you may have a volunteer deliver books to your house. Do you prefer to have your books:

_____ Mailed   _____ Delivered

Once your application has been processed, you will be contacted by a staff member to develop a personal reading and book delivery profile. You will be given your own library card and will be responsible for all materials checked out to the card. If you are a minor or under age 18, your legal guardian will assume this responsibility.

I have read the above information and qualify for at-home library service. I understand that I am responsible for all books I receive as part of the program.

Applicant's signature:_____   Date:_____

Guardian's signature (if for a minor):_____   Date:_____

TO BE COMPLETED BY YOUR PHYSICIAN, SOCIAL WORKER, OR REHABILITATION COUNSELLOR

I certify that the applicant requesting home library service is home- or institution-bound and unable to travel to the library.

Name:_____   Title:_____

Office/Agency Name:_____

Office/Agency Address:_____

Office/Agency Telephone Number:_____

Signature:_____   Date:_____

confirmation is important, as it relieves staff members from having to make independent judgments of patron need.

Security concerns and the need to protect both patrons and staff members dictate that at least two staff members should go to each delivery site. Many of the problems which may arise can be eliminated or mitigated by having two people present, and the peace of mind is well worth the extra expense.

Signs of Abuse and Neglect

It is possible that when performing individual outreach to a patron, you will see signs that the patron is being abused or neglected. In some states, there may be a law requiring that you report such suspicions. But even when you are not held legally accountable for failure to report any evidence of abuse, you do have a moral responsibility to do something.

If you suspect that a patron with a disability is being abused or neglected, explain the situation to your supervisor. In some areas, there are special agencies devoted to investigating possible elder abuse or child abuse. In others, the local police department or social service agency should be called. It is important to let the library manager know, because the manager may be responsible if any case such as this leads to legal action.

PROBLEM: Staff members become so involved with patrons that they become surrogate social workers, running extra errands or doing extra tasks more appropriate to a personal aide than to a librarian.
SOLUTION: Keep a strict delivery schedule. Go to more than one site each morning or afternoon, so that there is no time to perform this type of task. If you are a friend of a patron, you can visit after hours and run errands at that time.

PROBLEM: Personal outreach staff members become "burned out" because of intense involvement with individual patrons.
SOLUTION: Assign two people to each location, and have all outreach staff members meet regularly. These sessions should provide an opportunity to vent concerns and frustrations, and should also help brainstorm more effective and satisfying ways of providing service.

PROBLEM: People who are not disabled attempt to obtain personal delivery.
SOLUTION: Politely refuse delivery to all but those who have had applications approved by library management. Tell interested people how to apply and send them application forms. Refer anyone with further questions to library management.
SOLUTION: If the person is approved, but the staff member discovers that the patron is not, in fact, home-bound, notify library managers and explain the situation. The manager should be the one to call the patron's physician to verify the disability. Library staff members are not qualified to diagnose a person's disability.

Bookmobiles

As word of the availability of library delivery spreads, demand may increase to the point at which existing staff members cannot meet the community's need. High demand is likely to occur in areas which are not close to an existing branch. If significant numbers of people live in outlying areas, a bookmobile may prove the best way to provide service to people with disabilities and their neighbors.

A library purchasing a bookmobile should ensure that the vehicle is wheelchair accessible. If an existing bookmobile can be modified with a lift or otherwise made accessible, it should be. In these cases, staff members can serve patrons with disabilities in much the same way they would at the library. The situation is not always this rosy, however, and library staff members should prepare to meet some potential challenges.

PROBLEM: A bookmobile is not accessible.
SOLUTION: Staff members should deliver books for the patron.

PROBLEM: The bookmobile is not accessible, and service is often provided on rainy days in open areas such as parking lots.
SOLUTION: Install an extendable awning on the bookmobile which will protect people from the elements.

PROBLEM: The bookmobile may not be left unattended, and patrons need books brought to them.
SOLUTION: Have two people staff the bookmobile so that one is free to serve patrons who cannot board the vehicle.

PROBLEM: Patrons offer to take books for a patron with a disability.
SOLUTION: Have a staff member take the books. Using other patrons puts the person with a disability in the position of having to depend on the goodwill of others for library service.

PROBLEM: A patron with a disability cannot get to the scheduled bookmobile site.
SOLUTION: If the distance is not too far, drop off books at the patron's house as the circuit is made.

PROBLEM: A bookmobile or personal delivery site is unsafe either because of crime, road conditions, or other reasons.
SOLUTION: Report the problem to the program coordinator and, if possible, visit the site with the administrator to point out the problems.
SOLUTION: If crime is a concern, have a security guard accompany the bookmobile. If there is no cellular phone or two-way radio on board, install one.
SOLUTION: If there is no safe way to provide service to a location, provide in-home access by alternative means, such as mail delivery.

Figure 4.5   REQUEST FOR DEMOGRAPHIC INFORMATION

In an effort to provide the best library services for all students, faculty and employees, we ask that you please complete this survey and return it to the library at your earliest convenience. We also ask that you make information about library services available to all students, faculty, and employees served by your office.

Have any students, faculty, or employees identified disabilities which will affect their ability to use the library?

Yes_____   No_____

If yes, please complete the following questions.

Please list the number of students, faculty, and/or employees who have the following needs. Feel free to "double count" people who would benefit from more than one type of adaptive aid.

_____   Visual impairments requiring computer screen and book magnifiers

_____   Visual impairments requiring voice recognition software, screen readers, or Kurzweil- type reading machines

_____   Visual impairments requiring Braille materials or Braille computer displays

_____   Hearing impairments requiring assistive listening devices (excluding hearing aids)

_____   Hearing impairments requiring sign language, oral, or other interpreters

_____   Any impairments requiring special assistance by library staff members.

Please explain:

_____   Any impairments requiring other assistance or equipment.

Please explain:

Thank you for taking the time to complete this survey. Please return the completed survey to:

Applications for the
National Library Service
for the Blind and Physi-
cally Handicapped may
be obtained from your
state library or by writing
to the National Library
Service.
  National Library Service
  for the Blind and Physically Handicapped
  The Library of Congress
  Washington, DC 20542
  telephone:
  202-707-5100 (voice).

Books by Mail

When personal service is impossible, mail delivery of books is the next best thing. Of all outreach services, mail delivery presents the most minimal demands per patron on staff members. For this reason alone, library managers may choose to implement this type of outreach even when no other outreach to individuals is planned. The National Library Service for the Blind and Physically Handicapped and its member libraries throughout the country have provided mail services for a long time with great success. These libraries focus on materials for people who cannot use traditional print formats and need books on tape or in Braille. Public libraries do not need to duplicate the services of these libraries. Instead, they should keep NLS application forms available and assist patrons in completing and mailing them.

Libraries which plan to implement mail service, then, should focus their efforts on those people who prefer a traditional print format but are unable to come to the library. A few guidelines for service will help ensure effective mail service.

- Install a text telephone in the department which will handle the mail delivery service. If this is impossible, cross-train staff members who work in the department which does have text communications so that they know the mailing policies and can help patrons who call in queries or requests using a text telephone.
- Set clear check out periods and fine rules and advertise them clearly. Because mail delivery times can vary, we recommend using the postmark date as the final arbiter in the event of a dispute.
- Allow staff members some flexibility in overriding fine limits, but impose a written limit beyond which any leeway must be granted by the library manager.
- Refer any patron who argues a charge or delinquency to the library manager. Staff members should not have to mediate this type of dispute.

SPECIAL CONSIDERATIONS FOR SCHOOL AND ACADEMIC LIBRARIES

Academic and school libraries may provide specialized outreach service to students, faculty, and employees with disabilities. This is especially true when certain areas of the collection are not fully accessible. The decision about whether books will be delivered to a person's office or dorm room or simply to an accessible area of the library must be a matter of policy, and not left to the individual whim of staff members. Consistency of service provision in the most integrated setting possible should be the driving force behind these policies. Some basic guidelines will help library managers prepare an excellent service plan.

- Contact the school counselor or coordinator of services to students with disabilities at the beginning of each semester. Leave brochures about library service access in the counselor's or coordinator's office and send copies to students who have registered with the office. Include both new and returning students in the mailing.
- In school libraries which offer "parents' corners" or other similar programs, be sure to ask counselors about any parents or guardians who may have disabilities. Include these families when mailing out information about adaptive library services.
- Contact the personnel office at regular intervals to receive information about new faculty or employees with disabilities. Send information about available adaptive services to new constituents and leave brochures in the office.
- Advertise accessible services on school-sponsored radio, television, and print media through both articles and advertisements. Remember to advertise in faculty, employee, and student outlets.
- Post information about accessible services on school-sponsored electronic networks. If the library has a gopher or web site, work with systems staff members to develop a thread for patrons who want information about these services.

CONCLUSION

No matter how accessible transportation becomes, there will always be people who are unable to travel to the library. Outreach services ensure that these patrons continue to have access to library information. Providing outreach services can be demanding and time-consuming. But outreach can also be one of the most rewarding types of library service, as it engenders a very personal bond between staff members and patrons. By carefully preparing services, consistently serving the same clients, and following carefully considered procedures for handling difficult situations, we can maximize the richness of this experience for all involved and eliminate many of the difficulties.

RESOURCES

Alloway, Catherine, editor. *The Book Stops Here: New Directions for Book-mobile Service.* Metuchen, NJ: Scarecrow, 1990.

Alloway gathers together essays dealing with various aspects of bookmobile service. The authors discuss broad policy issues and provide practical information.

Casey, Genevieve M. *Library Services for the Aging.* New Hamden, CT: Library Professional Publications, Shoe String Press, Inc., 1984.

Casey's book focuses on older adults, and the chapter on nursing home service is not an exception. While some of the demographics are becoming dated, this chapter successfully combines a compelling philosophical argument for services to people in institutions and practical tips for ensuring their success.

Ring, Anne M. *Read Easy: Large Print Libraries for Older Adults. Planning Guide, Operations Manual, Sample Forms.* Seattle, WA: CAREsource Program Development, Inc., 1991.

This guide was developed primarily for use in establishing autonomous libraries in nursing homes and senior centers. Most of the suggestions and issues are readily adapted for use by all librarians and staff members for people who are institutionalized or homebound, regardless of the patron's age. The section on "using your public library system" suggests ways in which libraries may cooperate.

PROGRAMMING

Programs are often the most exciting and vital services our libraries offer. They introduce users to the collection, present literature of all types to all ages, or present how-to-do-it information on topics ranging from submitting a thesis to fixing a car. Making these programs accessible to all patrons, regardless of disability, is possible with a little foresight, and the rewards for both the library and patron are immeasurable.

LIBRARY WORKSHOPS AND EVENTS

Most library programs are just that, programs developed and run by library staff members and held in library facilities. These may include special events such as author visits, recurring programs such as book discussion groups, and workshops on topics ranging from conducting on-line research to auto repair. There are some general rules of thumb which apply to all types of libraries.

- Advertise, advertise, advertise.
- Practice using any special equipment on a regular basis.
- Request advance notification of patron needs.
- Be honest with the patron.
- Use as many formats as possible when presenting information.
- Videotape everything whenever practical.

Advertising

Unless patrons know about your program, they will not come. This is as true for patrons with disabilities as it is for anyone else. But patrons with disabilities also need to know that they will have the accommodations they need to benefit from library programs. In addition to regular program advertising, librarians should be sure to cover all bases to reach the community of patrons with disabilities.

- Advertise any accommodations (i.e., sign language interpreters, captioned or described videos, etc.) which will be available at the program.
- Include a brief notice which requests that individuals needing special assistance call the library to make arrangements as part of any advertising.
- Ensure that all staff members who may answer questions about the program are aware of planned accommodations or the procedure for obtaining special assistance.

When advertising a program, library staff members must remember that many patrons with disabilities are not regular library users. Advertising techniques must go beyond flyers left in the library or notices included in library newsletters.

- Advertise programs in multiple formats. Blind patrons are more likely to hear word of a program announced on radio or TV than in print, but radio announcements are less effective in reaching the deaf community.
- If your library runs a regular public access television program, include upcoming events as one segment of that program.
- Recognizing that some television viewers may be deaf or hearing impaired, be sure any information in a videotaped announcement is also printed on the screen either as a caption or simply as a screen of information.
- Post information on local computer bulletin boards to get the word out to non-traditional patrons. If the library itself does not have this type of access, ask staff members who have home computers to post notices of library events over their home computers.
- Add organizations for people with disabilities to the library's mailing and contact lists and send advance notice of upcoming events.
- When contacting agencies or organizations, give ample lead time so that they will be able to forward the information to their members.

Advertising should not end before the program begins. Signage within the library which clearly directs patrons to the meeting or program area is essential, and should follow a general format.

Directional signs should stress function over form. Dark block letters on bright white or light paper will serve patrons better than glittery swirls of fancy calligraphy. Letters should be 3" high, large enough to be seen clearly without being so large as to be confusing.

If an easel is used to support a sign, it should not obstruct the clear route of traffic.

- Include the name of the program, its time, and its location.
- If more than one turn is involved, install abbreviated intermediate signs with helpful arrows to guide patrons along the route.
- Remember to include the words "all welcome" whenever that is the case; this will encourage spur-of-the-moment attendees and put at ease those who have brought attendants or interpreters with them.
- Print all signs in large dark letters on a white or light background.

Advance Notification of Patron Needs

Arranging for sign language interpreters and set-up of adaptive equipment requires advance notice. Library flyers should clearly advertise how far in advance patrons must register for a program or provide notification of special accommodations which may be necessary. The deadline should be at least one business day before the deadline for hiring interpreters or renting equipment. Staff members should be able to take timely requests for most accommodations directly from the patron as part of the regular registration procedure. The sample "request for accommodation" (page 80) log can be modified to fit local needs and library resources.

If a patron indicates that special adaptations will be required, all staff members involved with the program must be aware of who and what will be involved. Advance planning will save staff members and patrons alike from having to decipher plans at the last minute. Completing a task delegation sheet which does not neglect after-program concerns will prove a useful tool to ensure accommodation efforts run smoothly. When problems come up, honesty is the best policy.

PROBLEM: A patron makes a non-standard accommodation request.
SOLUTION: Inform the patron that someone will call back to confirm. Do not tell patrons that an accommodation is not available. It is possible that the patron's needs can be met using an alternative adaptation. Refer the patron's request to the library manager or ADA coordinator.
SOLUTION: Do not promise an accommodation which may be impossible to meet. Simply take down the request, give the name of the person who will call back, and refer the patron's problem to that person.

PROBLEM: A patron calls 24 hours in advance of a program requesting a sign language interpreter, and the service requires 48 hours advance notification.
SOLUTION: Explain the advance notification policy and inform the patron that while every attempt will be made to secure the desired accommodation, it is possible that the search will not be successful. Take the pertinent information and refer the problem to the library manager.

When You Must Make Last-Minute Accommodations

Remind the patron of your notification policy for providing accommodations, but do not summarily dismiss the patron. Even if

Do not attempt to substitute a staff member who knows sign language for a qualified sign language interpreter. Interpreting is a specialized skill which involves a different type of fluency and training than simple communication. If a qualified sign language interpreter is not available for a program, the patron should be informed so that other arrangements may be made.

When programs involve specialized knowledge or jargon, familiarize the interpreter and the patron with the terminology before the program starts. The interpreter and patron may want to devise special signs so that translation is not slowed or missed because of unexpected terminology.

Because the library will have to pay for an interpreter whether or not the patron who needs interpretation actually comes to the program, it is a good idea to confirm program attendance with the patron before the cancellation deadline for the service. A quick reminder call to the patron can save the library a lot of money if it turns out the patron will not be coming to the event.

Figure 5.1   REQUEST FOR ACCOMMODATION

PROGRAM TITLE:_____

PROGRAM DATE:_____

REQUESTED ACCOMMODATION:_____

_____

DATE OF REQUEST:_____

REMINDER: If less than two business days' notice was given for contracted services or equipment, remind the patron that while the library cannot guarantee that we will be able to make the requested accommodations, we will do our best to arrive at some arrangement which will allow the patron to participate to the fullest extent possible in the program. Refer patrons with additional questions or concerns to the department head.

PATRON'S NAME:_____

PATRON'S PHONE NUMBER:_____VOICE/TDD (Circle One)

ACCOMMODATION ARRANGED:_____   BY:_____

ACCOMMODATION AND PATRON ATTENDANCE CONFIRMED:_____

BY:_____

If the requested accommodation was not available, list other alternatives offered and patron's response:

Figure 5.2   ACCOMMODATION TASK DELEGATION SHEET

PROGRAM NAME:_____

PROGRAM DATE:_____   TIME:_____

ACCOMMODATION REQUESTED:_____

TO DO:	PERSON RESPONSIBLE:	DATE DUE:	DONE?
Complete accommodation log			
Contact translator or other aide			
Arrange for adaptive equipment			
Confirm patron's attendance			
Confirm accommodation arrangements			
Arrange seating			
Hook up adaptive equipment			
Test adaptive equipment			
Test lines of sight for interpreters			
Greet patron and aide or interpreter			
Instruct patron in use of adaptive equipment			
Sign any invoices			
Disconnect equipment and clean up			
Other:			

your last-minute solution for providing access is not perfect, it may be enough to allow the patron to participate in the event. Here are some ideas for providing last-minute accommodations; think creatively to add your own solutions as well.

- Ask patrons sitting by an aisle if they would switch with a patron who has a guide animal so that the animal will have a place to sit and lie down.
- If seats are strictly reserved, wait until the end of the first intermission, then allow the patron and aide to sit together in unclaimed seats.
- If the library is not busy, recruit a staff member or volunteer to take notes for a patron who cannot hear the presentation.
- If the library is not busy, recruit a staff member or volunteer to describe visual portions of a program for a patron who is blind or visually impaired.
- If a patron can read large print, run off copies of handouts on an enlarging copier.

PROBLEM: A walk-in patron requests an accommodation.
SOLUTION: Have a last-minute procedure list on hand. Explain the advance notification requirement, but make every attempt to make some accommodation for the patron. If, for example, a sign language interpreter is not available, it might be possible for someone to take notes on the program.
SOLUTION: Have last-minute accommodation ideas worked out in advance and readily available to all staff members. This can prevent misunderstanding, deflect anger away from library staff members, and increase staff members' confidence in dealing with emergencies.

Adaptive Aids

Many libraries buy expensive adaptive equipment only to find it gathering dust. In some cases, this might be because there are very few patrons who would benefit from the device; in other cases it is because staff members or library managers unwittingly discourage use of the aid, either by putting it in an obscure location or not advising patrons of its availability. These problems may be addressed by following the guidelines offered in Chapter 1, "Library Orientation and Instruction."

Put your last-minute adaptive ideas here. Include information on staff members who know ASL or who may be able to help in other ways in a pinch:

_____
_____
_____
_____
_____
_____
_____
_____
_____
_____
_____
_____
_____
_____
_____

Poorly trained staff members will only compound the problem. Nothing is more frustrating to a patron than being "instructed" in using a library tool by staff members with no earthly idea how to use the tool themselves. The only way to combat this trend is to have library staff members routinely practice using the adaptive aids even if patron use of the equipment is low. Employees will be far more likely to encourage patrons to use equipment if they are confident that they can provide any needed assistance.

Practice is especially important when adaptive equipment is segregated in a separate locked room or is used infrequently, since it is frequent use which is most likely to make staff members comfortable assisting patrons. When equipment is kept locked away, there is often a certain staff member who is the guardian of the keys or the librarian in charge of the equipment. Much adaptive equipment is quite expensive, and there may be a reluctance on the part of the "guardian" to open the gates to other staff members on the grounds that the equipment is delicate or too hard to understand. Sometimes, politics and personal turf wars may come to bear on the decision of who learns to operate what.

This type of power play will prove most detrimental to the very patrons the library is trying to reach. All staff members need a working knowledge of the functions and capabilities of various aids. Such knowledge is vital for:

- **Referral.** Even if reference desk staff members are not allowed to assist patrons using special aids, they need to know what aids are available so that they can refer patrons to the proper department.
- **Reference.** Knowing how different aids work can also help reference staff members select the correct material. For example, if the library's only CCD magnifier is black and white, they might select maps with high contrast rather than those with colors with close gray values.
- **Bibliographic instruction.** Nowhere is familiarity with the workings of adaptive aids more important than in a program which teaches patrons how to use library tools. These are the keys to the library's collection, and a patron who does not feel comfortable using them will remain at a disadvantage.
- **Direct assistance.** Those staff members who might provide direct assistance in using adaptive aids will require a higher level of knowledge. If there are few patrons using a particular aid, the only way to get this familiarity is through practice and dummy sessions. Library managers should recognize this and encourage staff members to "play" with the adaptive equipment on a regular basis.

At programs which include audience participation, try to set up chairs in a semi-circle or "V" arrangement, rather than in straight front-facing rows. The curved arrangement helps people who rely on a speaker's visual cues for information.

If a sign language interpreter will be involved, ensure that there is a place for the interpreter to sit or stand that is close to, but not obstructing, the speaker. A good arrangement is to have the speakers on a dais with the interpreter in front at floor level. If possible, the patron and interpreter should have a chance to work out the best arrangement before the program starts.

Human and Animal Aides

Most library staff members know to make exceptions to "no animals" rules for seeing eye dogs for the blind. Staff members must remember, however, that guide animals are no longer limited to dogs, and the people they serve are no longer only the blind. Many people with severe mobility restrictions use dogs, monkeys, or other animals to retrieve items for them. Guide dogs may also be used by deaf patrons. Staff members should always ask before summarily ejecting an animal from the library. Of course, patrons with disabilities must follow the same rules as other patrons regarding non-working pets. Staff members can help patrons who use guide animals by remembering a few basic etiquette tips.

- If a patron will be attending a program with a guide dog or animal, be sure to reserve a seat for the patron which has room for the animal to lie down, either in the front or on an aisle.
- Allow the patron and guide animal to stay together throughout the program.
- Show the patron where to take the guide animal if it needs to relieve itself.
- Remember that guide animals are not merely pets, they are working companions. Do not attempt to stroke them, feed them, or otherwise distract them from their work.
- In the rare instance that a guide animal does become disruptive, talk to the owner. Do not attempt to separate the patron and the animal.

While some patrons with disabilities will use guide animals, others will be attended by human aides. Aides may be professionals, family members, or friends. Again, the patron and the aide should not be separated. Instead, extra seating adjacent to the accommodated patron's seat should be reserved for any assistant. If advance notice of the aide's attendance was not given, all effort should still be made to allow the aide to stay with the patron throughout the program. As in any other situation, employees should remember to address their remarks directly to the patron, not to the aide, even if the aide is also acting as an interpreter.

The Importance of Multiple Formats

Everyone appreciates handouts. They allow program attendees to carry home ideas that might otherwise be forgotten after an event. They enable program contents to be shared with those who were unable to attend. And, for people with learning or communications disabilities, they may ensure comprehension of a program while it occurs. For these reasons, we recommend that every library program, from basic orientation tours to involved subject-specific lectures, be accompanied by handouts which follow these general guidelines.

If you cannot afford to have separate brochures designed and printed in large type, use an enlarging copier to make inexpensive large print copies.

- Include the name of the program, date, presenters, and sponsors as appropriate.
- Use a minimum number of clear type styles in a typeface large enough to read, or print separate copies in a larger type font.
- Use a clear, uncluttered layout with ample white space.
- Test brochures to ensure they are readable or legible when used with the library's assistive reading aids.

Every program should be presented in as many formats as is possible. Following three basic guidelines will allow people with different learning strategies and communications methods to benefit from the same program.

- Present programs that are accessible through more than one sense. At a minimum, program contents should be available by sight and sound.
- Make every effort to ensure that all patrons benefit from the program, even if strict translations or notes are not possible. For example, blind patrons might be allowed to handle artifacts included as part of an arts and crafts show even if touching is not usually allowed.
- Never assume a person cannot benefit from a program. Some programs may seem inaccessible to certain audiences, but it is the patron who must make the final decision. Do inform patrons of the nature of programs. But unless participation by the patron will cause a direct threat to the safety of others, do not exclude the patron from a program.

Videotaping Events

One way to bring a program to patrons who may otherwise be unable to benefit from it is by videotaping the event. Videos provide both a visual and an oral record of the program which patrons can access at their own speed either at the library or in their own homes. If a library can arrange to have a videotape captioned and/or described, accessibility will be further enhanced. A local high school or community college may have a television or video

Before videotaping participatory events such as book discussion groups, get the permission of the people in the group. Explain that the videotape is being made so that patrons who cannot attend may still benefit from the discussion. Keep the recorder mounted on a tripod and placed as unobtrusively as possible. If participants are uncomfortable with being videotaped, the program coordinator should respect their wishes.

I'm an academic librarian—why should I care about story time?

Many academic libraries have story times, held under the banner of literature or poetry readings. As with public and school library story times, these may be accompanied by music, films, art displays, and demonstrations. Academic librarians may have to be more creative about what they call movement activities or visual aids, but almost every adaptation appropriate for public library programs will also work to improve the accessibility of academic library functions.

department through which volunteers may be found to run the cameras. If such help is not available, recruit a library staff member (with a tripod) to capture the event.

Make videotaping a routine for programs presented by library staff members. When guest speakers are presenting work, however, their permission should be sought first (page 87). Professional speakers may restrict the taping and rebroadcast of their programs. Explain that the program will be taped solely for the purpose of making the program available to people whose disabilities prevented attendance. Speakers who still refuse to be videotaped should have their wishes respected.

Public Access TV

Most cable TV companies run a public access channel which provides a free outlet to community groups with programs to air. Libraries can take advantage of public access TV to provide programming to home-bound patrons. Public access television may also be used to bring readers advisory services to patrons' homes through regular call-in book discussion programs. Libraries may look to public access television as an inexpensive advertising tool; its benefits as an adaptive aid should not be neglected.

STORY TIMES—FOR CHILDREN OF ALL AGES

One of the most popular programs at public libraries is story time. Story time provides an introduction to literature to young children and a way to enjoy books and stories for people who are unable to read. Typical story programs consist of more than a person reading from a book; they may include movement activities, multimedia presentations, music, and films. Librarians with the vision to maximize accessibility of story times to all patrons, including non-traditional audiences, will find their efforts well rewarded.

Building Accommodations into Story Times

Many story time accommodations will be made in the same way as program accommodations—through patron notification and accommodation. But story times present the library with a unique opportunity to improve access simply through attention to structure. Some simple hints in structuring story times can help improve accessibility for people with disabilities while at the same time improving comprehension and program enjoyment for all attendees.

Figure 5.3   PERMISSION TO VIDEOTAPE EVENT

The Pleasantville Library routinely videotapes library-sponsored programs and events for use by our patrons who, because of disabilities or other reasons, cannot attend the programs. If you would like your presentation to be included as part of this service, please complete the form below. Thank you for your help!

PROGRAM TITLE:_____

PROGRAM DATE(S):_____

PRESENTER:_____

I hereby give the Pleasantville Library permission to videotape the presentation listed above. I understand that this videotape is being made solely for private use by library patrons and will not be used by the library for any other purpose without my express written permission.

PRESENTER'S SIGNATURE:_____

DATE:_____

SIGNED STORY TIMES

Signed story times should be just that—not interpreted story times. A signed story is told in American Sign Language (ASL) and has its own sense of rhythm, character, and plot. Signed stories for young children are usually very visual and can be understood even by children who do not know ASL.

- Present the same story in multiple formats. Thus, if a film of Rumpelstiltskin will be shown at the end of story time, be sure to read or tell the story of Rumpelstiltskin as part of the program. Young children love repetition and like to see stories they know. Older children and adults will benefit by looking at alternative ways the same story can be presented. And for patrons with learning or communications disabilities, the varied forms of presentation may better serve to convey the story's message.

- Use flannel boards, chalk boards, puppets, or other visual aids when telling a story. Some storytellers rely heavily on voice and intonation to convey characters or other story elements, and these nuances can be lost on listeners with hearing impairments. Additionally, stories with complex plots or numerous characters may become confusing to some listeners. Visual aids can help listeners keep track of characters and plots so that they do not lose the thread of the story.

- At the same time, do not forget to tell the audience what is going on. Some storytellers use their body language or physical placement to convey characters. People with visual impairments will miss these clues. They will also miss the point of flannel board, chalk board or other visual stories unless the actions on the board are described as they are performed.

- Try to incorporate as many different types of presentation as possible into each story time. Rather than having five puppet stories one week and none the next, try to vary the methods of presentation.

- Have regular story time "anchors" to clue patrons in to what will come next. This may include singing the same song at each story time closing, doing a stretching activity at the same point each week, or having a standard "waiting" activity to keep patrons occupied while latecomers are seated. Use these anchors even when a guest will be doing the actual story time presentation.

- Be sure that the storyteller is well lit and can be seen by the entire audience. People with hearing impairments may rely on the storyteller's facial expressions and actions to fully benefit from the program.

- Ensure that any motion activities incorporate head, arm, and leg movements so that patrons with restricted mobility will still be able to participate.

These simple adaptations can be built in to every story time for any audience. If additional adaptations such as signed story hours or story times for visually impaired patrons are being offered by the library, advertise them heavily at specialized locations (such as schools or agencies which serve people with disabilities) as well as in print, television, and radio announcements. Remember that story times designed for non-traditional audiences must be advertised through media which will reach people who may not regularly visit the library.

Multigenerational Story Hours

Many libraries segregate people by age during story time. Those which do should also offer an all-ages story time, open to all. Multigenerational story times have several benefits which can be maximized with some advanced planning.

- Do not segregate seating, with children together in one place. This way, children who must be attended by a parent or aide will not feel stigmatized; the same is true of adults whose children act as aides or interpreters.
- Incorporate movement activities and songs or chants into the story time program. Encourage all attendees to participate.
- Present stories which "work" for both adults and children on various cognitive levels; they will appeal to adults and adolescents who have learning disabilities.
- Call the program "stories for all ages" or something similar, rather than "family" story time. This welcomes adults who do not have children but who could benefit from the program.

Adults-Only Story Times

Many libraries are initiating "adult" story times, offering tales from stories too scary or complex to be appropriate for young children. Adult storytellers tend to eschew visual aids, such as puppets or flannel pieces, and are less likely to include participation, especially physical participation, as part of the program, since it is assumed that adults are too "mature" to enjoy this type of presentation.

The enduring popularity of ventriloquists, magicians, and other entertainers gives the lie to this attitude. Adults may be reluctant to admit it, but they love puppets, props, and well-executed visual aids as much as young people. Storytellers preparing adult presentations may have to make their aids more sophisticated and may have to practice more to integrate the visuals into the story,

Here are three good sources on multigenerational story times.

Barkman, Donna. *Learning from the Past: Using Bi-Folkal Productions in School and Intergenerational Settings*. Madison, WI: Bi-Folkal Productions, Inc., 1992.

Bi-Folkal kits are popular multimedia kits (videocassettes, sometimes scratch and sniff, train whistles, paper hats–you name it) used in reminiscing programming with older adults. The theme-centered kits include discussion and activity guides and all materials needed for a program. Barkman discusses the possibilities and gives tips for using these kits with children and mixed-age audiences.

Bauer, Caroline Feller. *Caroline Feller Bauer's New Handbook for Storytellers: With Stories, Poems, Magic, and More*. Chicago: American Library Association, 1993.

Anyone who has watched a presentation by Caroline Feller Bauer knows that stories appeal to people of all ages. Bauer shares her considerable experience and creativity in this new handbook, which includes stories, ideas for presenting them, and specific instructions on assembling and creating props. Her book includes bibliographic references and an index for easy use.

Rubin, Rhea Joyce. *Intergenerational Programming: A How-To-Do-It Manual for Librarians*. How-To-Do-It Manuals for Libraries Series, No. 36. New York: Neal-Schuman Publishers, Inc., 1993.

Rubin provides a rationale for intergenerational programming, planning and evaluation guidelines, and program models, including story and reading programs, family literacy projects, story and program kits, history programs, theater and arts programs, and discussion programs. Included are useful worksheets, sample documents, and suggestions for additional resources. Especially useful is the list of program manuals, including complete addresses.

but they will still find the aids helpful in improving enjoyment of the presentation. Visual aids may help adult patrons with certain learning or communications difficulties and will be especially useful when presenting material to seniors who may be losing hearing or short-term memory.

Taking Story Hour Beyond Library Walls

As discussed above, public access TV and videotaped library programs can help spread the library programming to audiences who would otherwise be unable to participate. Story time programs also present an opportunity for staff members to personally visit other locations. Volunteers to help take story time "on the road" may be found among local community service organizations, schools, and colleges. Academic libraries may gain new audiences by hosting readings at area coffee houses or other gathering places. While mobile story times will help patrons whose disabilities prevent them from attending library events, their primary benefit to the library may be as an ongoing promotional effort.

READING CLUBS—FOR SUMMER OR ALL YEAR LONG

A Word About "Special" Reading Categories

Some libraries sign up reading club participants who have disabilities in special categories. The rationale is that this is a more "fair" arrangement for children with developmental disabilities who do not read as quickly or at the same level as others. But the inescapable implication is that these children put in less effort than their "normal" peers. This view is both false and self-defeating.

Reading programs are not pie eating contests or downhill slaloms, and in almost every case it makes the most sense to allow all patrons to participate in programs in the most integrated setting possible. The goal, typically, is to read a certain number of books or complete an independent course of study. Format preferences and reading level should not alter this goal.

If a program is specifically designed to promote print literacy, then by all means require patrons who are able to use print to do so. But remember that the "literacy" of patrons who use adaptive equipment or human readers to get their information from print is also being enhanced through program participation.

Reading clubs and contests are regular staples of public and school libraries. Some academic libraries also sponsor reading or book discussion clubs, but reading clubs are usually reserved for younger children. Because of the structured direction reading clubs take, all types of libraries should look at them as a way to reach patrons, especially those with disabilities, of all ages.

When a reading program is established, organizers often give little thought to including patrons with disabilities in their plans. Then, when patrons with disabilities want to sign up, staff members are unprepared, and problems creep up.

PROBLEM: Staff members are reluctant to sign up patrons who cannot use traditional print media.
SOLUTION: If specific books will be required, be sure they are available in alternative media (large print, tape, Braille, etc.) before adding them to the required reading list.
SOLUTION: If the media program is operated under the auspices of your state library, check to see if the state library has materials to help make the program accessible to patrons with disabilities.
SOLUTION: Allow materials obtained through the National Library Service for the Blind and Physically Handicapped or other sources to count toward the reading goal.
SOLUTION: Allow materials read to the patron, viewed on video, or listened to on tape to count toward the reading goal.

PROBLEM: An older child wants credit for a reading record composed entirely of picture books or easy readers.
SOLUTION: Allow material at all reading levels to count toward the goal, no matter how old the patron. Do not pass judgment on what reading level is appropriate for a particular child.

Extending the Reading Program Concept

As noted above, reading programs are often confined to summer public library promotions aimed at school-age children. Extending reading programs across all ages and through all seasons is good for all, but especially for patrons with disabilities for many reasons.

- Patrons with certain disabilities may have lower educational levels and can benefit greatly from directed learning programs which allow them to continue their education independently.
- Patrons with learning disabilities may find that a directed program fosters greater understanding and allows them to broaden their reading interests across disciplines.
- Reading programs for teens and adults which include group discussion periods or presentations provide an opportunity for patrons with disabilities to socialize with non-disabled community members who share common interests.
- At the same time, these discussion periods introduce non-disabled patrons to people with disabilities on a personal basis.
- Reading programs which take format availability into account prevent the frustration of being unable to follow a course of study because certain materials are not available in needed formats.
- Ongoing reading clubs or plans encourage new people to join the program either on an open basis or at regular intervals. Some patrons with learning disabilities will benefit most from these plans, which allow readers to proceed at their own pace.

With attention to material and format selection, you can develop a plan which promotes the library and literacy to all patrons with a minimum of extra staff effort and time.

Craft and How-To-Do-It Programs

Libraries often offer hands-on how-to-do-it workshops. In an academic library, the focus may be on research or writing. In a public library, holiday crafts or car repair may be the focus of the event. Staff members may be reluctant to sign up people with disabilities to participate in these programs for a variety of reasons. By structuring programs to anticipate likely concerns, program coordinators can produce meaningful workshops which are as inclusive as possible.

- Print instructional handouts in clear type. Give examples on the handouts, or draw pictures to show various stages in a step-by-step activity.
- If the program participants will be making something, prepare a finished copy of the item in advance for participants to use as a model. If the steps are complex, models showing the item at intermediate stages will be helpful. Allow participants to view and handle the models while they are working.
- If a program requires certain talents such as fine motor skills or extremely good visual acuity, say so in the promotional literature and ask those who may need assistance to call the library in advance. Do not, however, prevent patrons with disabilities from attending based on your own judgment of how much benefit they would derive from the program.
- If an instructional video will be shown, try to get one that is captioned. Turn the captions on even if nobody has requested them, especially with adult programs. Adults who have beginning hearing loss may be reluctant to mention it or may themselves be unaware of it, and providing captions as a matter of course will help improve comprehension for all.
- Provide assistance to any patrons who need it. If patrons registering for a workshop note that they have limited motor control or some other disability which may prevent full participation, offer to provide an aide to help them with the project or craft.
- Allow aides to attend programs without "counting." For example, if a workshop is limited to ten people, the patron and the aide should count only as one participant.
- As a rule of thumb, double the amount of time you think program participants will take to complete a task when first estimating program length. This will prevent the program from being rushed, which may frustrate people who need a little more time to finish a task.

These basic program modifications should help ensure that all programs are accessible to all patrons. Because everybody has a slightly different learning style, even patrons without disabilities will benefit from the increased attention to format and instruction.

OUTSIDE ORGANIZATIONS AT THE LIBRARY

Libraries with meeting room facilities (and many without) often allow local groups to present programs or hold meetings in the library. For the most part, being certain that these groups welcome participants with disabilities falls to management, who must ensure that open access means just that. Of course, open access rules apply to groups representing people with disabilities as well as those which do not. Just as a group of sighted patrons could not prevent a blind person from attending a program or meeting, a group of blind patrons should not be allowed to exclude sighted people from its programs.

Stopping Problems Before They Start

A carefully worded meeting room policy (page 95), application plan, and resource sheet can help prevent these problems. There are three basic questions all outside groups petitioning to use the library should be asked.

- Does your organization limit membership in any way? How?
- Does your organization plan to limit attendance at library programs in any way? How?
- Library patrons with disabilities may wish to attend your meetings or programs. Have you previously worked to accommodate attendees with disabilities? Are you willing to provide such accommodation?

To further avoid problems:

- Develop a meeting room agreement which includes a statement on participation by people with disabilities.
- Clearly describe any adaptive aids the library may be able to provide to outside groups, and explain the procedures for reserving such equipment or services.
- Review the policy when groups first apply to use the library so that there will be no later misunderstanding.
- Enforce non-discrimination policies when groups are unwilling to make reasonable accommodations to allow patrons with disabilities to attend.
- Recognizing the importance of lead time to arranging for accommodations, require reasonable advance notice to reserve a room. This will eliminate the charge that groups are using last-minute room reservations to circumvent the need to provide access to patrons with disabilities.

Even with advance planning, there will be snags. Problems which do crop up for staff members to handle can be anticipated and mitigated by proper staff involvement.

PROBLEM: The library has a policy of open access to any meetings held in the library. A support group for people suffering from a certain disease complains that people who are not members of the group are sitting in on meetings.
SOLUTION: Explain the policy on open access which was part of the agreement the group signed. If the group still complains, refer the contact person to library management.

PROBLEM: A patron calls requesting a translator or other aid for a meeting sponsored by an outside group.
SOLUTION: Refer the patron to the group's contact person.

PROBLEM: A group contact person calls requesting that the library arrange for a translator or other aid for a meeting the group is sponsoring.
SOLUTION: Explain the policy in the meeting room agreement stipulating that when outside groups sponsor events held in the library's meeting space, it is the group's responsibility to provide accommodation.

ONE SAMPLE POLICY FOR MEETING ROOM AGREEMENTS

The Pleasantville Library wishes to remind organizations using library facilities that they are responsible under the Americans with Disabilities Act (ADA) for providing interpreters or other aids for patrons who have disabilities. The library will assume financial responsibility for these arrangements when a program is sponsored by the library itself; in other cases, it is the responsibility of the organization holding the meeting or event to pay for interpreters, equipment, or other accommodations. Organizations signing this agreement signify their willingness to honor this policy. The Pleasantville Library maintains a list of interpreters who can be contacted by organizations. The library may also be able to lend adaptive equipment to organizations, provided that the equipment is not needed for a library-sponsored program or event. Any such arrangements must be made at least two business days prior to the event.

SOLUTION: Provide a list of any adaptive aids the library may have in house which can be reserved by the group.
SOLUTION: Provide the contact person with a list of local translators or aid providers.

PROBLEM: A patron shows up at the last minute for a meeting or program sponsored by an outside group and requests accommodation.

SOLUTION: Help the group contact try to make emergency accommodations to the greatest extent possible.

SOLUTION: Explain advance notification procedures to the patron to prevent future misunderstanding.

PROBLEM: A group refuses to make a program or meeting accessible.

SOLUTION: Explain the library's policy on open access. If the group still refuses to allow the patron to participate, refer the group's contact and any patron with a complaint to the library manager. Write up the incident and report it to the library manager.

CONCLUSION

One of the biggest fears associated with serving patrons with disabilities is that it will be impossible to accommodate all patrons at library programs or events. While it may be impossible for every library to provide every type of adaptive aid or service, in most cases we can use a few inexpensive devices and common sense to make programs accessible to the broadest possible audience. This should be your goal when planning any type of library workshop, program, or event.

RESOURCES

Berliss, Jane, editor. *Adaptive Technologies for Accommodating Persons with Disabilities.* Special issue of *Library Hi Tech* 11, no.1 (1993).

This special issue, devoted to adaptive technologies for people with disabilities, provides an excellent overview, explanations of technical processes, and descriptions of existing services in selected libraries. The level of discussion is accessible to most readers, regardless of whether they are "tekkies" or technophobes, and most articles deal with service and policy issues as well as more technical matters.

Hagemeyer, Alice L. *The Legacy and Leadership of the Deaf Community: A Resource Guide for Librarians and Library Programs.* Chicago: ASCLA/ ALA, 1991.

Hagemeyer, a pioneer in library service to the deaf community, has contributed a number of important works to library literature over the past two decades. This resource guide will prove valuable for those trying to expand programs and services to the deaf and people who are hearing impaired.

Jahoda, Gerald. *How Do I Do This When I Can't See What I'm Doing? Information Processing for the Visually Disabled.* Washington, DC: National Library Service for the Blind and Physically Handicapped, The Library of Congress, 1993.

Jahoda's excellent book provides an introduction to assistive devices, computer technology, and adaptive techniques for people who are blind or visually impaired. He also provides topics for programming for this clientele, as well as resources to support collection development and programming.

Mates, Barbara T. *Library Technology for Visually and Physically Impaired Patrons*. Westport, CT: Meckler, 1991.

Mates provides an excellent foundation for exploring library technology for people with disabilities. Because of the rapidly changing nature of technology, however, it will be necessary to supplement this basic text with more recent information.

Mayo, Kathleen and Ruth O'Donnell, editors. *The ADA Library Kit: Sample ADA-Related Documents to Help You Implement the Law*. Chicago: ASCLA/ALA, 1994.

Mayo and O'Donnell have compiled an extremely useful collection of documents to serve as models for libraries expanding services to people with disabilities. The documents include community surveys, policies and procedure documents, transition plans, materials for staff training, accessibility statements, and brochures and fliers from 14 public and university libraries.

National Library Service for the Blind and Physically Handicapped. *Story Hour at the Public Library: Ideas for Including Visually Impaired Preschoolers*. Focus on Children Series. Washington, DC: Library of Congress/NLS, 1988.

The NLS provides guidelines and practical strategies for ensuring that visually impaired children can participate fully in story times in the most integrated setting.

6 SPECIAL NEEDS OF CHILDREN AND YOUNG ADULTS

This book takes a holistic approach to improving service to patrons with disabilities. It is important not to band people with similar disabilities together, because every patron and every patron's interest is different. However, all patrons' needs are the same—to access the programs and services they want and the library offers in the most fully integrated setting possible. There are some concerns, however, which are unique to children and seniors, and it is to these concerns we address in this and the following chapter.

SERVING CHILD AND PARENT

Parents of children with disabilities can sometimes seem to be especially protective of their children. Some parents may recognize that their children can create special demands on staff and try to be as helpful as possible. Others may have to act as aides or interpreters for their children. Still others may simply be fearful of leaving their children alone. Staff members should try to understand a parent's motivations when they believe the parent may be diminishing the quality of a child's library experience.

- Ask the parent if there are any special needs the child has of which staff members should be aware.
- A parent may try to protect a child from insensitive or hurtful remarks. Be accepting and open to the child (speaking to the patron, not the disability) to reassure the parent that your goal is to provide the best service to the child.
- Explain that you would like to talk directly with the child, even if the parent must interpret, because it allows the child to think through the question. Explain the importance of one-on-one communication in building library research skills.
- Reassure parents that you are aware of the extra demand on staff members' time, and that you appreciate their willingness to lend a hand.
- If the parent is not strictly needed, but is reluctant to leave the child, have another staff member take the parent a

short distance away where the child can still be observed. This staff member can then explain to the parent what is going on, and the child will be able to interact with library staff members independently.

- Have something for the parent to do while the child looks for books. The parent may wish to remain in the children's floor or section, so keep some books on parenting, homework help, or other related topics on hand.

Some libraries are actively re-thinking "children's only" programs and are encouraging attendance by adults and caregivers.

There are still some programs or occasions when it is beneficial to the child to interact unselfconsciously with the librarian and other children, but without parent/caregiver at programs.

- Parents who are needed as aides or interpreters should attend an otherwise children's-only program. If attendance is limited, count both parent and child as one participant. If the parent brings another sibling along, however, that child must meet the program requirements.
- Parents who are not needed as aides or interpreters should not attend children-only programs. Reassure these parents by explaining that if children need to leave the program for any reason, they are brought to their parents right away. Encourage the parents to talk with other people who bring their children to library programs.
- Some parents may be afraid of the reaction of other children to their child. Ask them if there is anything they can suggest to help with this. Some parents may want to introduce the child to the other attendees and explain the disability in matter-of-fact terms; if so, allow them to do this.
- If there is a place parents can go to observe the child without being seen by the child or disrupting the program, allow parents to do this until they are reassured that their children are benefitting from the program.

SERVING YOUNG ADULTS WITH DISABILITIES

Young adults with disabilities have special concerns when negotiating the maze of adolescence. At an age at which many people feel alienated to begin with, teens with disabilities may shoulder the added burden of being the only person they know "like them." Other teens with progressive terminal diseases may be watching their friends die and wondering if they will be next. Still others will be worried about the "normal" questions of sexuality, popularity, and life after high school.

Library staff members can help teens with disabilities by keeping up-to-date resources handy.

- Keep bibliographies of books, videos, and tapes, both fiction and non-fiction, which feature other teens with disabilities.
- When college-entry materials (such as SAT test booklets) come in, read them to familiarize yourself with the application procedures students with disabilities must follow.
- Keep a list of computer bulletin boards teens can join. People can interact electronically at their own pace and do not have to reveal their disabilities unless they want to.
- Keep a list of Internet resources and support groups for people with disabilities. In some areas, these may provide a teen's only access to others who have the same disability.
- Do not be misled into believing that physical or mental disability precludes sexuality. If the library offers teen-oriented brochures on these issues, be sure they are available in alternative formats.
- March is Disabilities Awareness Month. Use this month to promote biographies of people with disabilities.
- Remember that family, friends, and schoolmates can be a great support to teens with disabilities. Keep materials and referral sources on hand to help this non-disabled support group stay informed.

SELECTING BOOKS FOR CHILDREN WITH DISABILITIES

Library staff members are not bibliotherapists. Nonetheless, staff members should be able to recommend books to help children understand and cope with a disability. Some guidelines will help improve readers' advisory services to children; the section on readers' advisory in Chapter 2 will also provide helpful guidelines.

- Look at the person, not the disability. Children with disabilities have the same questions, concerns, and interests as their non-disabled peers.
- Remember that deafness, blindness, and physical disabilities do not impair cognition. Do not assume that children with these disabilities are reading below grade level. Ask them what books they have read and enjoyed, and find them similar materials.

THE "RULE OF 5" FOR JUDGING READING LEVELS

Author's Note: This "folk" rule for judging whether a book is appropriate for an individual was taught when I was in graduate school in education. Years later, the same rule resurfaced as part of a library science class. I have found the method to be a useful off-the-cuff tool when selecting books for both children and adults.—CD

1. Take the book in question and open it to a random page. Make sure the page is not the first or last page of a chapter, and that it is a text page (if there are illustrations on every page of the book, use two facing pages for the test).
2. Ask the patron to read the page silently, holding up one finger whenever there is a word that is difficult to read or understand. Be patient and allow the patron to read at whatever pace is most comfortable.
3. Judge the appropriateness of the book by the number of fingers held up at the end.

5 or more	The book is probably too far above the patron's reading level and would be very frustrating for the patron to read. If the patron is interested in the story or topic, the book might be a good choice for a read-to-me selection.
3–4	The book is probably above the patron's reading level. If the patron is very interested in the story or subject, it may still be a good choice, especially if the book has good illustrations. If the patron is not very interested in the story or subject, the book will probably be too frustrating to be enjoyed.
1–2	The book is a good choice. The patron's vocabulary will probably improve, since one or two words can usually be deciphered in context without too much frustration. The book may also be a good teaching tool, since if it is read with someone who has a more advanced vocabulary, unfamiliar words can be explained.
0	The book is probably at or below the patron's reading level. This does not mean it is a poor selection. Easy reading material builds confidence and helps reinforce skills and comprehension. Further, many people, especially children, enjoy reading favorite books over and over. Some parents are reluctant to check out books that are below grade level or otherwise "too easy" for their children. Remind them that while some books should be a challenge, there is no harm in a few light reads.

- Use the Rule of 5 as a quick guide to selecting books at the child's reading level if it is not known. Teach parents how to use this rule—it is a great off-the-cuff tool.
- Prepare a bibliography of books owned by the library which address different disabilities using some of the special bibliographic review tools mentioned. Review incoming acquisitions and update the list accordingly.
- Some topics, such as integration of deaf or blind children into "regular" schools, are quite controversial. Do not attempt to guide parents or children to one point of view or another.
- Do not censor material given to children with disabilities. If a book is worthy of being included in a collection, it should be worthy of recommendation to all. Would a librarian choose not to recommend "A Christmas Carol" to a child who uses a leg brace because of its stereotyped

portrayal of Tim Cratchet? Books and libraries do not exist in a vacuum, and it is no more appropriate for librarians to "protect" children with disabilities from negative stereotypes than it would be to keep girls from reading any book which stereotypes women.

- On the other hand, be alert to outdated books, especially non-fiction works, which are biased, unfair, or represent outdated thinking. For example, a book which talks about opportunities for people with physical disabilities only in terms of sheltered or home-based work is probably outdated and should be replaced with a more current and accurate portrayal of career options.

Special Tools for Readers' Advisory for Children with Disabilities

Staff members who will be providing readers' advisory to children with disabilities will find specialized reference books helpful. We list several below which may be particularly valuable.

CONCLUSION

Almost all program concerns which apply to adults apply to children as well, but serving children with disabilities may offer special challenges to library staff members. By having bibliographies and other resources on hand, ensuring fair access to all materials by children with disabilities, and remembering that it is the child, not the parent, who is the patron, library staff members will have the tools to provide excellent service at their fingertips.

READER'S ADVISORY GUIDES FOR CHILDREN

Carlin, Margaret F., Jeannine L. Laughlin, and Richard D. Saniga. *Understanding Abilities, Disabilities, and Capabilities: A Guide to Children's Literature*. Englewood, CO: Libraries Unlimited, 1991.

Carlin, Laughlin, and Saniga provide an annotated bibliography divided by disability into nine chapters. Each chapter includes information on books and films. Each annotation includes bibliographic information, a literary merit symbol (*,**,***) and a symbol to denote appropriateness of portrayal (+ or −).

Friedberg, Joan Brest, June B. Mullins, and Adelaid Weir Skiennik. *Portraying Persons with Disabilities: An Annotated Bibliography of Nonfiction for Children and Teenagers*. New Providence, NJ: RR Bowker, 1992.

An update of *Accept Me As I Am, Portraying Persons with Disabilities* (nonfiction) provides an overview of trends (past and present) in literature about people with disabilities, a discussion of selection criteria, and a chapter of reference books as well as an annotated listing of selected works. The bibliography is arranged alphabetically by author within major topic categories (physical

problems, sensory problems, cognitive and behavioral problems, and muliple/
severe problems). Each entry provides bibliographic information, reading level,
review source, disability subject heading, a summary of the work, and an *analysis* section. This is a companion volume to Robertson (below) and is arranged
in the same manner.

Libretto, Ellen V., compiler and editor. *High/Low Handbook: Encouraging
    Literacy in the 1990's*. 3rd. NY: RR Bowker, 1990.
    Libretto's book contains several chapters of particular interest to those serv-
ing young adults with disabilities: "The Disabled Adolescent Reader," "The
Promise of Computers," and "High/Low Books for the Disabled Reader." In
addition, she offers general purpose advice on selecting and evaluating high/
low materials. Each entry includes bibliographic information, a subject heading, reading level (by grade), and interest level (by grade). The subjects covered vary greatly–from date rape to learning to be a supervisor to biographies
of famous sports figures. Author, title, and subject indexes are provided.

Robertson, Debra. *Portraying Persons with Disabilities: An Annotated Bibli-
    ography of Fiction for Children and Teenagers*. 3rd. New Providence, NJ:
    RR Bowker, 1992.
    Continuing in the tradition of *Notes from a Different Drummer*, Robertson
provides an annotated bibliography for use in reader's advisory for children
and young adults with disabilities. In addition to the bibliography are chapters on trends and a professional resource list. The bibliography is arranged
alphabetically by author within category (physical problems, sensory problems, cognitive and behavioral problems, and multiple problems) and Donavin
includes author, title, and subject indexes as well. Each entry has bibliographic
information, reading level, review source, disability heading, summary, and
an *analysis* section. This is a companion volume to Friedberg, Brest, and Mullins
(above) and is arranged in the same manner.

RESOURCES

Programming for Serving Children with Special Needs. Library Service to Chil-
    dren with Special Needs Committee, Association for Library Service to Chil-
    dren, American Library Association. Chicago: ALSC/ALA, 1994.
    Produced by a committee of ALSC, this brief work (19 pages) is a revised
edition of the 1981 publication of the same name. Very focused and specific,
it gives practical advice for programming for children with disabilities.

Schuler, Carolyn, and Susan Meck. "Sharing Traditional and Contemporary
    Literature with Deaf Children." pp. 61–84 in *Libraries Serving an
    Underserved Population: Deaf and Hearing-Impaired Patrons*. Edited by
    Norton, Melanie J. and Gail L. Kovalik. *Library Trends* 41 (Summer 1992).
    Schuler and Meck outline ten considerations in choosing and sharing lit-
erature with deaf children: selection and presentation, emotional needs of the
child, images of the culture, basic time frames, child's preparation, access points
to the story, versions and translations, literalness and levels of interpretation,
illustrations, and didacticism. They discuss the significance of each of these

factors to deaf children. In addition, they provide practical tips for more effective storytelling.

Walling, Linda Lucas, and Marilyn H. Karrenbrock. *Disabilities, Children, and Libraries: Mainstreaming Services in Public Libraries and School Library Media Centers.* Englewood, CO: Libraries Unlimited, Inc., 1993.

This is the single best source for providing services to children with all types of disabilities. Meticulously researched and clearly presented, the descriptions of types of disabilities, their characteristics, and effects on cognitive and perceptual abilities provide library staff with the understanding necessary for providing excellent service. Walling and Karrenbrock provide important practical information on collection development, programming, and communication and offer an extensive resource list.

Walling, Linda Lucas, and Marilyn M. Irwin. *Information Services for People with Developmental Disabilities: The Library Manager's Handbook.* Westport, CT: Greenwood Press, 1995.

This unique source is essential for librarians who want to gain a better understanding of patrons with developmental disabilities. Walling is joined by Irwin, whose extensive experience at the Center for Disability Information and Referral at the Institute for the Study of Developmental Disabilities (Indiana University) is apparent in this work. Of particular interest to those serving children and youth are chapters on early intervention and education, toys and games, methods for sharing literature with developmentally disabled children, and the role of the school media center in serving youth.

7 SPECIAL NEEDS OF SENIORS

As we age, we are likely to develop disabilities ranging from poor vision and hearing to loss of mobility to mental impairment. Often, these disabilities set in gradually and go unrecognized for a long period of time. As an example, while 29 percent of older adults have a hearing impairment, only 8 percent use a hearing aid (U.S. Bureau of the Census. *Statistical Abstract 1988*, 1987, p. 110 in Vierck, Elizabeth. *Fact Book on Aging*. Santa Barbara, CA: ABC-CLIO, 1990, p. 100). The unique nature of disabilities in senior patrons has implications for all who serve this segment of the community.

ANTICIPATING OLDER PATRONS' SPECIAL NEEDS

The fact that disabilities in older people set in slowly and may go unrecognized makes anticipation of patron needs all the more important. Staff members can help by making a few preparations and following basic etiquette rules.

- Treat older adults as adults. They have the experience and knowledge of a lifetime.
- Respect older adults as individuals and recognize that there is a great diversity within the older adult population.
- Remember that many patrons enjoy the social as well as the informational aspects of a visit to the library. Develop closure techniques to end reference interviews with tact and grace.
- If books are stacked on high or low shelves, provide seating or secure step stools which will allow patrons to reach the books they need independently.
- Advertise the availability of aids such as magnifiers or text readers in or near the large print collection and the reference desk.
- Erect signs at OPACs and computer terminals which direct patrons who need assistance to help desks.
- Follow the same rules of communication outlined in Chapter 1 when helping older patrons, even if they do not "look" as though they have a disability.

Following these rules will help minimize problems serving older patrons, many of which can be anticipated.

An excellent policy guide for service to seniors is available free to libraries.

"Guidelines for Library Service to Older Adults," Prepared by the Library Services to an Aging Population Committee. Reference and Adult Services Division. American Library Association. Adopted January 1987. *RQ* 26 (Summer 1987): 444–447. Also available from RASD and on the ALA Internet site (gopher:/ /gopher.uic.edu/11/library/ ala)

Two sections (sections 2 and 4) of the guide illustrate its inclusive, policy-oriented approach:

2. Promote information and resources on aging and its implications not only to older adults themselves but also to family members, professionals in the field of aging, and other persons interested in the aging process.

4. Provide library service appropriate to the special needs of all older adults, including the minority who are geographically isolated, homebound, institutionalized, or disabled.

PROBLEM: A patron does not seem to be able to hear you, but says there is nothing wrong with her hearing.
SOLUTION: Follow the basic rules for patron communication. Keep your face lit; do not let your hair, hands, or anything else block your mouth; do not eat, drink, or chew gum; and speak clearly in a normal tone of voice.
SOLUTION: Write down information as you give it to the patron. This ensures that the patron will receive the correct information even if you are misunderstood.

PROBLEM: A patron complains about the type in a book, but becomes insulted when the staff member suggests that he select material from the large print collection.
SOLUTION: Steer patrons to "regular" books with large print features. Some "regular" print books are printed in almost microscopic type; others are printed in a font very close to "large" print size. Large print size usually ranges from 14 to 18 points, and 12 point books with ample line spacing may provide a very near approximation to this standard. Ample line spacing can also make a "regular" print book easier to read.
SOLUTION: Suggest books which match the patron's reading interests but which are available only in large print. In this way, you can introduce the large print format in an entirely non-pejorative manner. Once the patron is accustomed to the large print format, initial prejudice against it may dissolve.
SOLUTION: Integrate large print and regular print collections for popular titles and new acquisitions, even if the regular collections are segregated.
SOLUTION: If large print books are shelved separately, be sure they are in an easily accessible, prominent area of the library.

PROBLEM: A patron complains about the weight or bulk of large print books.
SOLUTION: Suggest newer editions. Improvements in paper thinness have led to a marked reduction in the bulk and weight of large print works. At the same time, the new paper is more opaque than its predecessors, preventing the annoying bleed-through that was sometimes a problem with large print.

PROBLEM: A patron cannot remember whether or not he has read a particular book.
SOLUTION: If the book has a book card used in outreach, write the patron's name on the card so that in the future you will know who has read the book.
SOLUTION: Encourage the patron to keep a reading log. This will

also help if the patron wants to read books in series, especially when more than one author has contributed to the series.

SOLUTION: Have the patron devise a system for reading, either by working through a suggested reading list and crossing off titles as they are read, or simply by starting at A and working to Z.

PROBLEM: A long-time patron suddenly seems to be dissatisfied with library services and/or reading material.

SOLUTION: Work with the patron, family members, or aides to do the best you can for the patron. Give the patron "tried and true" authors which the patron has enjoyed in the past.

SOLUTION: Give the patron more books. This increases the chances that some of them will be of interest.

SOLUTION: Do not take a patron's rejection personally, and do not generalize this behavior to all older adults. Keep a sense of humor and perspective, and focus on the books that the patron did like, rather than those that were rejected.

PROBLEM: Patrons who once attended the library independently now come with aides or caregivers, who select materials based on their own tastes, not the patron's.

SOLUTION: Remember to talk to the patron when conducting the reference interview, not the caregiver or aide.

SOLUTION: If the patron will not communicate or is sending the caregiver alone, talk to the caregiver. "I'm surprised your father is reading mysteries; he usually checks out westerns," is a tactful way to introduce the subject. The caregiver may be unaware of the patron's reading habits.

PROBLEM: A patron cannot come to the library any more, and the library does not offer individual outreach services.

SOLUTION: Allow aides or relatives to come to the library to select books for a senior patron who cannot make it to the library.

SOLUTION: Get the patron's request for books by note or phone and have the books checked out, bagged, and waiting when the aide or relative arrives.

SELECTING BOOKS FOR SENIOR PATRONS

Some patrons lose their cognitive abilities as they age, a process which can be extremely frustrating and demoralizing. Patrons who begin losing the thread of complex plots or involved arguments present a special challenge to library staff members who are trying to serve them. Some basic techniques can help library staff members who are choosing books for these patrons.

Too racy for whom?

The daughter of an elderly patron complained to the library staff member:

"Those books you gave my mother were too racy. She doesn't want anything like that. She just wants a good clean love story."

Rather than explain that it was the mother who had selected the books, the staff member nodded, smiled, and mm-hmmd politely but non-committally until the daughter left. Fifteen minutes later, the mother appeared, books in hand. They were the same type of erotic thriller she normally checked out.

"Are you sure that's what you want? Your daughter was here a few minutes ago, and she said this wasn't really the type of story you wanted."

"Oh, yes. Thank you for reminding me," said the patron. She picked up a medical romance which was on display. "This," she said, poking the book a few times for emphasis, "is for *her*."

Remember that publishers often follow gender-specific lines when classifying books. For example, coming-of-age novels about males are often classified as "adult" books, while similar books about females are considered "young adult" novels. Many readers of all ages like this type of novel, especially those that focus on interrelationships among multi-generational family members or deal with larger issues of morality and life experiences. If you serve older patrons, be sure to maintain ties with your counterparts in the young adult section to keep abreast of new works which would be of interest to your older patrons.

Creative Education has issued a very well-produced set of individually bound classic stories. Although the set is intended for young adults, the covers have more mature artwork and the books, although not "large print," have a typeface which is large and well-spaced enough for most large-print users to be able to enjoy.

- Consider a format change from print to audio materials. Remember, however, that "regular" tape recorders may not be suitable for certain patrons. Blind or severely impaired patrons may not know that a tape is entangled in the machine and may inadvertently damage audiotapes; people with loss of motor control may find a regular tape player difficult to use. Refer these patrons to the National Library Service for the Blind and Physically Handicapped (NLS); the special equipment used by the NLS is specifically designed for use by people with these types of disabilities.

- Select stories which are episodic in nature and which have clear chapter and section divisions. These stories are easier to read and return to in "chunks" without losing the narrative thread.

- When selecting books for non-fiction readers, choose those with maps, photographs, and illustrations which appear alongside the text to which they refer.

- Consider well-written young adult or children's books. Many books now considered "young adult" were in fact written for adult readers, but are housed in the young adult collection because they frequently appear on school reading lists. Classic books such as *The Secret Garden* or *The Incredible Journey* may appeal as much to adults as to children, and are written in language which will not insult the intelligence of the adult reader.

- Suggest short story anthologies. Some anthologies are actually designed to come together as a whole, which may make them more enjoyable to patrons who do not generally like short stories. Others profile the same person or locality, again making them good choices for people who prefer a more "novel" approach to their reading.

- Consider individually rebound editions of short stories. These may be housed in the young adult or children's section, although they are reprints of classic adult short story authors such as Capote, Cather, Dickens, Jackson, and Poe. The individual binding of the short story gives it the feel of a novel, and, because the publisher is stretching a short story to go into a book, the print is usually large and generously spaced.

CAREGIVERS AND FAMILY MEMBERS

Increasingly, adult children are serving as caregivers to their aging parents. They may also be working and have families of their own. Library staff members can help these caregivers immeasurably by implementing a few aids.

The library should be a place where caregivers can find materials which will help provide respite and renewal for their day-to-day tasks. Respite can often be found in the form of light popular fiction: keep a display of works in all genres available. Renewal can be aided by information which will help caregivers cope with and find support for their situations. Some suggested resources include:

Bensing, Karen McNally. "Rejuvenating Your Books on Aging." *Library Journal* (October 1, 1993): 55–58.
   Bensing's article demonstrates the value of using traditional resources to develop collections for special groups. *Library Journal* is generally already in use in the library and the materials featured are readily available and current. Bensing's list includes topics of interest to both older adults and caregivers and provides annotations and full bibliographic information. A nice plus is a listing of agencies and associations from which free or low-cost pamphlets may be obtained.

Brazil, Mary Jo. *Building Library Collections on Aging: A Selection Guide and Core List*. Santa Barbara, CA: ABC-CLIO, 1990.
   Brazil's section on "Caregiving" provides complete bibliographic information and annotations on books for caregivers. Included are such works as *The Unfinished Business of Living: Helping Aging Parents Help Themselves* and *Parentcare: A Commonsense Guide for Adult Children*. Also recommended are books that focus on families of older adults, for instance, *Women Take Care: The Consequences of Caregiving in Today's Society*. Audiovisual resources, journals, and newsletters are described. Useful resources will be found in other sections dealing with specific and diverse issues in aging, such as alcohol and drug abuse, Alzheimer's disease, elder abuse, employment, ethics and legal issues, health, housing, intergenerational relationships, leisure, or technology.

Donavin, Denise Perry. *Aging with Style and Savvy: Books and Films on Challenges Facing Adults of All Ages*. Chicago: ALA, 1990.
   Donavin's annotated bibliography lists both fiction and nonfiction works. Arranged alphabetically by author within topic, this book includes a single subject-author-title index. Included are sections on family relations (including a substantial section on assisting aging parents); health, fitness, and sex; grieving, death, and final arrangements; travel and recreation; housing; retirement; biographies and memoirs; humor and reflections; poetry; plays and films; and fiction. Donavin's list of associations includes such diverse groups as Elder Craftsmen, The Gray Panthers, and the American Heart Association.

Rubin, Rhea Joyce. *Of a Certain Age: A Guide to Contemporary Fiction Featuring Older Adults*. Santa Barbara, CA: ABC-CLIO, 1990.
   For those who find wisdom and support through fiction, Rubin's book is invaluable. Two basic criteria for inclusion in this annotated bibliography were that the central characters were 55 years old and older and the novel or story was first published in 1980 or after in English. Each entry includes bibliographic information, a theme heading, and an evaluative summary. If the work is available in an alternative format, that is noted at the end of the entry. The well-conceived and structured indexes (author, title, thematic, genre, and alternative format) make this a delightfully simple work to use. Caregivers will be particularly interested in works listed in the thematic index under "Adult Children of Aging Relatives" and "Family Relationships," together with appropriate "see also" references.

- As noted above, if caregivers will simply be picking up books for the patron, have the books checked out and ready to go to save time.
- Keep a display of information of interest to caregivers (brochures from support groups, books on caring for aging parents, etc.) in a location near the large print collection or in other areas frequented by senior patrons.

CONCLUSION

As with all other patrons, the key to providing excellent service to seniors is careful planning. The attitudes necessary to provide the best service can only follow from the confidence gained through training, practice, and experience and backed up by a policy which provides staff members with both guidance and support. When we work with aging patrons, we must remember that, as with all patrons, we must focus on each patron as an individual. By doing so, we promote a climate in which excellent service to all will be the norm.

RESOURCES

Casey, Genevieve M. *Library Services for the Aging*. Hamden, CT: Library Professional Publications, Shoe String Press, Inc., 1984.

Although this work is becoming dated, it provides an excellent conceptual base for working with older adults. Initial chapters on the demography of aging and the intellectual competence of older adults provide important arguments for service to this clientele. Practical guidance in chapters on library service in nursing homes, education for library service to the aging, and planning public library service to the aging are still valuable and pertinent.

Hudson, Elizabeth A. *Libraries for a Lifetime*. Oklahoma City: Oklahoma Department of Libraries, 1989.

Libraries for a Lifetime is a manual in the vein of Rubin and McGovern's *Working with Older Adults* (see below). Hudson's work is a bit more current and extensive, and has specific sections on "working with the impaired elderly," "tips for working with the impaired elderly," and "do's and don'ts for communicating." Extensive resource lists are provided.

Ring, Anne M. *Read Easy: Large Print Libraries for Older Adults. Planning Guide, Operations Manual, Sample Forms*. Seattle, WA: CAREsource Program Development, Inc., 1991.

Ring's manual offers a simple step-by-step guide for establishing and maintaining libraries in nursing homes and senior centers. Included are resources and ideas for working with older adults.

Rubin, Rhea Joyce, and Gail McGovern. *Working with Older Adults: A Handbook for Libraries*. 2nd. Sacramento: California State Library, 1988.

Rubin and McGovern's manual is an excellent planning guide for training and for developing services. Compiled in a looseleaf binder, materials are clearly and carefully presented for quick reading and easy reproduction for staff and volunteer training. Checklists, samples of public relations materials, and resource lists simplify the process of providing service.

Turock, Betty J. *Serving the Older Adult: A Guide to Library Programs and Information Sources.* New York, R.R. Bowker, 1982.

Turock continues to be an advocate of services to older adults and has produced a number of valuable studies since *Serving the Older Adult* was published. The first three parts of this original work, however, provide a combination of ethical consideration, gerontological background, practical service models, and planning methods that have not been equalled.

8 THE IMPORTANCE OF TRAINING—WHAT FRONT-LINE STAFF MEMBERS CAN DO

Ask most people with disabilities to name the biggest barrier to equal service and they will answer with one word—attitude. The best written policies and most up-to-date adaptive equipment will only gather dust if employees do not foster a sense of welcome to all people and encourage them to use the equipment. But staff members are not likely to feel comfortable with either patrons or technology if they do not receive proper training. In fact, thoughtful on-going training is probably the most important single tool to improve service available to library managers, and it is often available free or at very little cost.

FORMAL TRAINING SESSIONS

Any Americans with Disabilities Act (ADA) service training plan should begin with formal training sessions. While formal training sessions involve more effort on the part of planners and presenters, they have some definite advantages.

- Paid speakers will reach the most employees for the least cost in a full-group or large-group setting.
- Large group sessions build camaraderie, allowing staff members who might not normally work together to meet and exchange ideas.
- Formal sessions emphasize the library's commitment to the training program and the goals of excellent service provision.
- Formal training is usually highly structured and can be repeated without excessive variation in quality.

Formal training does, however, have some drawbacks which must be recognized.

- Cost can be high, especially if the session must be held outside the library.
- If an important speaker cancels, the results can be a nightmare.

- Scheduling formal training for all library employees may mean having to close the library for an in-service day.
- Very small libraries may not have the staff members to justify on-site formal training, especially where speaker/trainer fees are involved.

Service excellence is possible only when the library as a whole demonstrates a commitment to all constituencies. Squeezing in informal training segments when the library isn't busy conveys the clear message that the training isn't really important. The logical conclusion is that the object of the training isn't important, either. Even if the bulk of training has to be informal, the ADA program coordinator should schedule at least one big formal session to build morale and a sense of service commitment.

Large Group Training

Libraries which can afford to do so should offer both large and small group training sessions, but even in the largest settings all libraries should have at least one session with as many staff members present possible. Ideally, this would be the first training session and would include three elements.

Do not be afraid of a speaker saying bad things about library services, so long as the speaker is being factual, rather than vindictive. Remember that the purpose of the training program is to improve service, and this can only be done when we recognize that service is *never* perfect to begin with.

Do, however, be wary of speakers from groups which have a specific, highly focused agenda. If a potential speaker, for example, talks about how the library needs to purchase one specific technological device to the exclusion of all other topics, this should send up a warning flag about the likely tenor of the full presentation.

- A short enthusiastic speech by the director in support of the program, focusing on the opportunity to expand services to patrons with disabilities who would otherwise be unable to benefit from library services. This is a far more positive and motivating message than one which talks about ADA compliance or legal obligation. Remember that the audience is staff members, not internal auditors.
- A second enthusiastic speech by the ADA or outreach services coordinator, outlining the goals of the department and any services currently provided to patrons with disabilities. This is a good time to share stories about actual patrons with disabilities who have benefitted from the library's programs for patrons with disabilities. If the library is a school or academic library, the coordinator for the school or university may also want to make a brief presentation about the demographics of the student population and any services offered by the school as a whole.
- Presentations by guest speakers representing community groups of people with disabilities. Guests should be asked to outline any special information needs of the groups they represent and should give advice on proper etiquette for serving patrons who have those disabilities. These presentations should be accompanied by hand-outs on common etiquette tips.

Of course, presentations will vary among libraries and may include more than these three basic elements. There are a few cautions to consider, however, when planning certain activities for large group sessions.

- Video presentations. Even with a large projection-screen TV, video presentations may not work well with large groups. The screen may be difficult for some attendees to see; the audio may not be intelligible to all. The large group setting may also make attendees wary of asking questions or discussing issues raised in the video, although in some large groups the result may be the opposite.
- "Sensitivity" exercises involving role playing. Use this technique, which can turn into more of a game than a learning experience, very cautiously. Blindfolding people or passing out ear plugs and wheel chairs in a large group setting may stress the carnival aspects of the exercise rather than fostering true sensitivity.
- Any kind of personal feelings/"sharing" experience. The likelihood of anyone admitting honest feelings about almost anything when in the presence of co-workers, the library director, and invited speakers is just about zero. The one person who does say something honestly felt is likely to be the one person who will mortify the director or insult an invited guest. This type of exchange is usually best for small, informal settings.

After the presentation, staff members may ask questions of the speakers. In larger settings the questions can be written down and handed to runners to save time and to consolidate related questions. Some "plants" may be solicited ahead of time to ask specific questions, avoiding the awkward feeling which may be engendered if nobody volunteers. Once the formal question and answer period is complete, the session can adjourn to an informal coffee-and-cake reception. This is especially useful if speakers with disabilities have attended, as it allows library staff members to become personally acquainted with these community representatives.

Small Group Presentations

In a small library, the full group presentation can be immediately followed by training which requires staff member participation. For libraries with staff size larger than 20 or 25, however, smaller groups work better for hands-on training. It is not within the scope of this book to present a full-scale training module. There are, however, several approaches to training.

- Hiring an outside expert to hold a training session for all staff members, or sending all staff members to outside training sessions.
- Sending key personnel to outside training sessions or hiring an outside expert to train these staff members, then having the key personnel train others.
- Having key staff members conduct all training using a purchased training module or one they have designed.
- Using self-guiding modules to allow staff members to train themselves.

Because every library setting is different, one type of training is not always the best. Library managers must consider the advantages and drawbacks of each approach in light of individual circumstances before reaching any conclusions about which route to take.

Formal Training for All Staff Members by Outside Experts
Advantages to formal training for all staff members are clear.

- Sessions are given directly by a qualified trainer so that there is no corruption of the information or presentation.
- All staff members get to view training videos or use auxiliary equipment which may not be available at the staff member's location.
- Because all staff members, regardless of rank, receive the same training, the importance of the project and the importance of front-line staff members to its success is emphasized.

There are some disadvantages to formal training.

- Outside experts cost money, and the cost will generally rise with the number of trainees. In small libraries it may make little difference, since group trainers usually charge a flat rate per session.
- Library staff members are "out of commission," a cost which must also be considered, especially if the trainees must be replaced by other staff members earning overtime.
- Scheduling may prove difficult if several people must be absent from a department or branch at the same time.

Training Trainers

One method of training which is gaining popularity is the training of trainers. In this system, a core group of employees attend a formal training session, then are assigned to train other staff members. This option has several benefits.

- Costs are lower, since only the core group receives training from a consultant or at a seminar.
- The core group may develop an increased sense of responsibility for the success of the program, since they are responsible for spreading the training.
- Core group members may tailor the information they have received to the specific needs of the library.
- Subsequent training sessions may be scheduled in a way that does not interfere with public service provision.

There are serious drawbacks, however, and library managers must give them full consideration.

- Many wonderful librarians and library managers are lousy trainers. Politics may dictate that the core group consists of managers and people most senior in the organization, regardless of their skills as trainers. This compromises the program.
- The people identified as core trainers may have the least amount of free time available to arrange subsequent training sessions.
- If training is viewed as a perquisite and some people are not given the opportunity to attend, animosity may build toward the program.
- Staff members of lower rank may not be accepted as trainers by their higher-ranking co-workers.
- The lack of a neutral party conducting subsequent training sessions may make people more reluctant to ask honest questions or voice concerns.
- Some supplemental material offered to the core group may not be available in subsequent in-house sessions. Training materials may be copyright protected, and videotapes or other aids may be unavailable.

Semi-Formal In-House Training

Some libraries which do not have the resources to hire outside consultants or pay for conference fees will opt to have training conducted in-house by a key staff member. The coordinator for

ADA compliance or services to patrons with disabilities will often take on this role. This approach has its merits.

- It is extremely cost-effective, since there are no outside consultants involved.
- Because the trainer comes from the library system, the course can address the library's specific needs.
- With only one person responsible for the program, training equity for all staff members is probable, and if that staff member is given official sanction to conduct the training, sufficient time must be set aside to prepare a thorough presentation.

There are pitfalls, however.

- If the designated staff member is a poor trainer, the entire program will be compromised.
- If the designated employee is given responsibility for training but not freed up from other duties, it may be impossible to develop and stick to a comprehensive training plan.
- Trainees may be unwilling to voice their true opinions and concerns to the staff member, especially if the staff member is part of the administrative unit.
- If the trainer is of low rank, other employees may not take the program seriously.

Informal Self-Guided Training

Self-guided training does have its place and has several advantages.

- It is the least expensive option, requiring only that the library purchase manuals or videos.
- Each staff member can move through a self-guided program at whatever pace is most comfortable.
- The library does not have to close or make any special arrangements to accommodate training.
- A self-guided unit is completely written out and can be used over and over again.

Of course, self-guided training has drawbacks.

- Staff members have no opportunity to get feedback on their ideas or to learn from the ideas of others.

- Employees working busy shifts may have little time to spend on the training materials.
- Training materials may become scattered, buried in a bottom drawer, or otherwise relegated to a back shelf.
- A do-it-when-you-have-a-chance system conveys the message that the training is definitely not a high priority. As noted earlier, the logical implication is that the service is equally unimportant.

Synthesizing Training Elements

In most situations, no one training method is best. Instead, a good training plan will synthesize many elements of each method into a single comprehensive program. An excellent training program will consist, at minimum, of the following:

- At least one large group training session to kick off the program, including speakers from the library and from the community.
- Some type of formal small group training for all library staff members. If this is not possible, a core group of trainees representing all departments and a variety of job levels should attend formal training, then be sent to train others.
- On-going follow-up training by the ADA coordinator, conducted on-site or in-department. These sessions should keep employees abreast of new technology and services and specifically emphasize their departments' importance to service excellence.
- Support materials including purchased or borrowed training videos circulated throughout the system. The ADA coordinator should also assemble basic reference materials to keep at each site so that individual employees can go through them at a comfortable pace. On-going hints and tips can be printed as part of the monthly staff newsletter, stressing the library's continuing commitment to disabilities awareness and service excellence.

New Staff Member Training

As new employees join the library staff, they will receive training in library policies and procedures. This training should include several elements related to services to patrons with disabilities.

- How to use any adaptive equipment.

- Basic rules of etiquette for serving patrons with disabilities.
- Information on the demographics of library patrons, especially if the library serves a large number of patrons with one or more disability.

Even if the new employee has one or more disabilities, this procedure should be followed, since not all people with disabilities are alike. The new staff member should also be given time to view any service training videos and complete any self-guiding exercises the library may have.

Training for Paraprofessionals

In some library systems, a clear demarcation is made between professional librarians and paraprofessional staff members. In these systems, it may not be "policy" to pay for training for paraprofessionals. Libraries who want to stress quality service must overcome this bias for several reasons.

- Paraprofessionals are very often front-line staff members. Patrons may not know that the people who are serving them are not "real" librarians.
- The purpose of training is to improve service to the patron. This means that everyone who serves the public should be trained, regardless of rank.
- Today's paraprofessional may also be tomorrow's professional librarian. Many library technicians or assistants go on to complete their masters' and move up in the system as librarians. By denying paraprofessionals training, library managers are putting their future librarians at an unnecessary disadvantage, and may also be denying them motivation to prepare for a full range of professional responsibilities.

Some Sensitive Caveats

"Sensitivity training" has become a common training technique where inclusion is the goal. The general aim of sensitivity training is to help build empathy—to make people think "how would I feel if . . . " In principle, it sounds wonderful, helping people to truly understand another group by simulating the conditions that other group must face. In practice, though, library managers should be very careful before attempting this type of training. When conducted crassly, or casually, sensitivity training may take on a carnival atmosphere, leading to little more than extreme discomfort of all involved. There are some ways, however, to help make sensitivity training worth the effort.

- If sensitivity training will be conducted by an outside consultant, be sure to get references before signing the contract. Ask previous trainees what the training entailed, how long it lasted, and what the general assessment of the program was. A warning flag should go up if the training involved aggressive tactics such as employee "hecklers" making fun of the participants with disabilities.
- Make sure the sensitivity segment is conducted in the library and that each participant's simulation lasts long enough (as much as a full day) to allow time to get past the novelty of the role.
- If possible, separate trainees to several locations so as not to overwhelm library patrons and non-participating staff members. In very large systems, the participants might want to go to locations where they are less likely to be recognized by other employees so that they will be treated as if they were patrons.
- Be sure to follow sensitivity sessions with a discussion of the activity. If possible, community representatives from groups representing people with the disabilities should be present to confirm, augment, or even criticize the experiences staff members had.
- Remember that sensitivity exercises focus on disabilities rather than abilities. Follow-up discussions and activities should make participants aware of what people with disabilities *can* accomplish.

Sensitivity training has a place in a balanced training program, but only if it is integrated into the entire training experience. It should never be conducted in isolation, and library managers should not agree to "sensitivity" training which simply dredges up and rehashes negative feelings and antagonistic stereotypes.

Soliciting Community Speakers

Many community advocacy groups provide speakers at no charge. Soliciting these speakers may involve little more than a phone call, but the library manager must do the proper homework to ensure that the speaker is a good one and that both speaker and audience will benefit from the experience.

- Investigate the focus of the advocacy group. Some groups are designed to foster community awareness, others advocate political action, and still others may be activist groups which form protests, etc. The focus of the group may be important in choosing from which a speaker will be solicited.

- Try to get a speaker who is a regular library patron. In an academic or school library, this might be a professor or teacher who will be known to many of the staff members. At the very least, the speaker should have some commitment to library services. Talk to the actual speaker about the speech and about libraries in general before making any final decision.
- Discuss fees up front. If the library does not have the funds to pay an outside speaker, say so. If there is money in the budget but it is not enough to cover the speaker's usual honoraria, explain the situation. People generally support libraries, and the speaker may be willing to waive or reduce the fees if asked. Don't ask, though, unless you have to; this type of organization usually operates on a very small budget.
- Ensure that the person is a good speaker. Ask for references as you would with any other speaker. If possible, attend a lecture or program given by the speaker before making a final decision.
- Ask in advance about any special arrangements the speaker might need for the program. These may include a sign language interpreter, a raised platform or a podium which can be raised and lowered (or taken away) to accommodate a speaker who uses a wheelchair, or a describer to help a speaker who has a visual impairment. If any speaker or attendee will be using a wheelchair, be sure that the facility (including rest rooms) is fully accessible. Do not take the word of facility managers; check out the site yourself to avoid unpleasant surprises.

Having speakers with disabilities talk to staff members will benefit both the training program and the library as a whole.

- Outside speakers give the program more visibility and credibility within the community of people with disabilities.
- Outside speakers are part of a network of people who can work with the library on focus groups or other efforts and who come to the program with a positive feeling about the library's goals and intent.
- Having people from the community speak may generate

Remember that knowing sign language does not qualify someone to be an interpreter. Sign language interpreters go through specialized training in the art of interpretation. Staff members who use sign language can communicate directly with patrons who also sign, but they are not appropriate translators for training programs or other library events.

QUESTIONS TO ASK WHEN SOLICITING COMMUNITY SPEAKERS

Always remember that the purpose in having a community speaker is to provide staff members with input from people who are or who represent patrons with disabilities. When these speakers offer their services free of charge, you may be tempted to accept them "sight unseen." Remember, though, that a poor speaker will do your program more harm than good. All prospective speakers should be interviewed before any agreements are made. Basic interview questions should address the speaker's goals and experiences.

What type of presentation do you give?

Be wary of speakers who say things like "whatever you want" or "it doesn't matter" or who are otherwise vague. Experienced speakers know their strengths and know what types of presentation best suit their speaking styles.

How long does your presentation usually last?

An experienced speaker should be able to give you a range.

Have you given this presentation before? When? To which groups?
If not, have you given other presentations before? When? To which groups?

If the speaker has only given presentations to groups with very different demographics (for example, school children) than are represented by your library staff members, make sure the speaker understands the change in audience. Take notes, write down the names of the groups the speaker mentions, and contact them. Check out references whenever possible. Do not feel that you are being insulting—good speakers appreciate having their credentials confirmed in this way.

Do you frequently use the library? How? (Try to get the speaker to expand on this.)

Basically, you are trying to discover the speaker's attitude toward libraries. Does the speaker see the library as a lifelong source for learning and leisure reading? Or is the library viewed merely as a tool for doing school reports? The ideal speaker would be familiar with the scope and range of library services and able to consider how library services to patrons with disabilities could be improved. Speakers who do not believe libraries are important are unlikely to be able to motivate library staff members.

What do you think are the greatest challenges faced by patrons with disabilities who want to use the library?
What are your suggestions for staff members who want to improve service to patrons with disabilities?

Once more, you are looking for speakers who are familiar with library services, who can identify areas in need of improvement, and who can think of positive ways to accomplish those improvements. For training purposes, it is important that the focus of improvements is on day-to-day measures which individual employees can implement (for example, increased awareness of patron needs). A red flag should go up if the prospective speaker talks only about physical barriers over which staff members have no control.

interest in the program from the press, which will further spread the word about the library's commitment to service.

- Having speakers with disabilities talk to staff members combats the idea that people with disabilities do not want to use the library. Knowing that there is a constituency out there which does want and need service is a great motivator.

ON-GOING TRAINING

On-going training keeps awareness high, ensures that staff members know how to use any new adaptive equipment, and provides time for employees to practice using equipment already on hand. Any library which has undertaken an excellent training project can keep the benefits going by using a few easy on-going training and awareness tools.

- Keep statistics on the number of people using adaptive equipment, and encourage patrons to contribute their analyses and suggestions. Print usage figures and positive stories in the staff newsletter.
- Advertise new materials and circulate particularly interesting ones to all branches and departments. For example, if the library has recently acquired a videotaped sign language course, send a copy of the tape around to each branch for staff members to look at.
- Send away for free brochures and circulate them before putting them into the vertical file.
- Leave extra copies of adaptive aid catalogs in the break room. They help bring to mind some of the day-to-day challenges and concerns people with disabilities have. They also help emphasize the things people with disabilities can do once an environment is accessible.
- Send the ADA coordinator to every branch and department on a regular basis to do a walk-through and talk with the staff members. This should not be a punitive "inspection," but rather an opportunity for staff members to voice concerns or make suggestions.
- Make timetables of ADA-related programs which will be held at conferences and encourage attending staff members to go to at least one of them. Conference attendees may have a block of time free that corresponds to an ADA program which they may not otherwise have considered attending.
- Encourage people to take sign language or other courses which may be offered through your institution or govern-

ing agency and provide them with time off to do so. Once staff members feel comfortable signing, a "sign language spoken here" sign or button can announce the availability of employees who can sign with patrons.

- Print hints and tips for improving service to patrons with disabilities in the staff newsletter. Include periodic instructional reminders on how to use equipment.
- Include notices of recent acquisitions about people with disabilities, both fiction and non-fiction, in the staff newsletter.
- Post the promotional displays and use some of the free awareness material given out in March, which is Disabilities Awareness Month. If your library does not participate in this activity, use the material anyway. Most of the material is suitable for use at any time.
- Route articles about service to patrons with disabilities to all staff members, not just department or branch heads.

CONCLUSION

A well-developed training program can be your best tool in keeping service excellence a priority. Training by outside consultants or internal experts can be combined with an aggressive and sustained on-going awareness campaign. The employee newsletter is an exceptionally powerful tool because it is read by almost everyone. It is often also distributed to trustees, friends, and other closely associated groups, who will recognize the library's continuing commitment to excellent service for all. Free training opportunities build morale while enhancing each employee's ability to serve all patrons. And circulating material helps keep everybody "in the loop" in terms of new developments, ideas, or service provision techniques. With so many opportunities available to the library at such a small cost, training can be used indefinitely to help make the library a positive force for change.

RESOURCES

Lucas, Linda. "Educating Librarians to Provide User Education to Disabled Students," pp. 97-114 in *Teaching Librarians to Teach: On-the-Job Training for Bibliographic Instruction Librarians*. Edited by Alice S. Clark and Kay F. Jones. Metuchen, NJ: Scarecrow Press, 1986.

Lucas (now Linda Lucas Walling) does her normal thorough job in organizing information for its maximum effectiveness providing techniques for teaching the teachers.

Mayo, Kathleen, and Ruth O'Donnell, editors. *The ADA Library Kit: Sample ADA-Related Documents to Help You Implement the Law*. Chicago: ASCLA/ALA, 1994.

Mayo and O'Donnell include staff training materials from four libraries (two public and two university) in this ASCLA sponsored monograph. Also included are copies of policies and procedures, transition plans, sample accessibility notices, and copies of accessibility brochures and fliers.

New York Public Library. *Making Contact: A Guide for Library Staff Serving Patrons with Disabilities.* n.d.

NYPL's pamphlet instructs staff in basic etiquette and service provision. Concise and straightforward, it touches on the main points and can serve as an excellent basic tool for staff training.

Sorenson, Liene S. *Accessible Library Services: Taking Action to Enhance Public Library Services for Persons with Disabilities.* Skokie, IL: Skokie Public Library, 1988. (Distributed by the American Library Association.)

Sorenson probably did not produce this document as a guide for staff training, but its clear organization and attention to all aspects of service can serve as a model to be adapted by other libraries in outlining staff training programs.

Systems and Procedures Exchange Center. *Library Services for Persons with Disabilities.* SPEC Kit 176. Washington, D.C.: Association of Research Libraries, 1991.

In addition to planning documents, service policies, and other pertinent documents, this SPEC Kit provides staff training materials from the University of Maryland. Materials offer guidelines on how to interact with people with disabilities, techniques for using TDDs, lists of appropriate and inappropriate vocabulary, and a copy of the Issues in Disability Scale. Do note that the instructions for use of the IDS assure complete anonymity. Many trainers prefer not to collect surveys at all, but to allow individuals to use them for personal awareness.

Wright, Kieth C., and Judith F. Davie. *Serving the Disabled: A How-To-Do-It Manual for Librarians* No. 13. New York: Neal-Schuman Publishers, Inc., 1991.

Worksheets, reproducible training materials, lists of audiovisual materials, and an instrument for measuring experience with disabled persons are provided by Wright and Davie, along with basic instructions, methods, and rationale for training. The advantage of *Serving the Disabled* over some other sources is in its thorough instructions and warnings about misuse of survey instruments and disability simulations.

Videocassettes (for use in training)

What Do You Do When You See a Blind Person? American Foundation for the Blind. 1971. 15 West 16th Street, New York, NY 10011.

The clothes, music, and cinematography of this film are dated, but it provides a wealth of practical advice for interacting with people who are blind. Some of the dated aspects (polyester clothes) are amusing rather than distracting and serve as icebreakers in a self-conscious group.

People First: Serving and Employing People with Disabilities. 1992. 40 min. Library Video Network, Baltimore County Public Library from ALA Video, 50 East Huron Street, Chicago, IL 60611.

Offered by the American Library Association, this video features conversations with people with disabilities and library staff members. Vignettes illustrate simple rules of etiquette that enhance library service.

9 SAFETY FIRST!

Disaster is a topic on which nobody likes to dwell, but it is important to be prepared so that if there is an emergency, it will not become a tragedy. People with disabilities are especially vulnerable to dangers of fire and other hazards. Some people may not be able to detect emergency warning signals. Others may not be able to negotiate stairways, fire escapes, or emergency routes. When preparing a safety plan, you should be sure that procedures for alerting people to danger and evacuating the building include provisions for those with disabilities. And should an emergency arise, you should feel confident that all staff members are able to escort patrons to areas of safety whether or not they have disabilities.

BEFORE AN EMERGENCY

There are some basic preparations which the library manager should have in place, whether the library is a one-room branch or a multi-story facility.

- Ensure that floor plans showing evacuation routes are clear and up to date. If construction or repair work has blocked an accessible exit route, post temporary evacuation route maps which show the path people should follow in an emergency.
- Designate one person per shift and per floor as the emergency coordinator, and another to act as back-up. These people should be aware of all rescue procedures and are responsible for ensuring the safe evacuation of their area in the event of an emergency.
- Designate an area of rescue assistance in all multi-story locations and in any location where some areas do not have an accessible means of emergency egress. If you are uncertain as to the location of this area, ask the local fire prevention officer to visit the building and point out the proper areas.
- Designate two reunion areas for all emergency coordinators. One should be outside, in case of a fire or other emergency in which a building must be evacuated. The other should be internal, for use during emergencies such as tornados or earthquakes in which people should remain inside. Even in a tiny branch, there can be great confusion during an emergency, so the meeting areas should be specific and not left to chance.

EMERGENCY SUPPLIES EVERY LIBRARY SHOULD HAVE

Emergency equipment should be clearly labeled and kept in an uncluttered, easily accessible location. Emergency supplies are just that, and should not be raided by staff members with paper cuts, etc. If your library serves a large number of patrons with disabilities, augment your emergency supplies accordingly.

On every floor or in each area of the library you should have:

Fire extinguisher (ABC type)
Basic first aid kit
Flashlights (at least two)
Scissors (the blunt-tipped "cuts-anything" kind are a good choice)
Evacuation sling (one for each floor)
Blanket
Diagram of any shut-off valves, etc. located on the floor or in the area
Plan indicating emergency exit routes, areas of rescue assistance, and reunion locations
Emergency procedure list, including people responsible for evacuation, etc.

In a main location:

All of the above items, plus:
A more extensive first aid kit
Staff roster
Master set of plans including locations of shut-off valves, areas of rescue assistance, and reunion locations.
Procedures for notifying the main site of any emergency if the site is a branch or satellite location.

- Keep an emergency kit containing an evacuation sling, face masks, and basic first aid material in a fire-proof location.
- Encourage employees to receive first aid and CPR certification and training in how to evacuate disabled individuals without injury to themselves or others. The Red Cross, institution or government department of safety, or local fire department may provide this training in your area at little or no cost.
- Ensure that new emergency coordinators are designated if a coordinator or back-up leaves or changes duty shifts or locations.

- Practice emergency procedures. Drills should be timed.

Staff members can also make preparations to ensure that an emergency will be handled calmly and effectively.

- Keep fire doors closed and emergency exit routes clear.
- Know who the emergency coordinator and back-up are every time you start a shift.
- Be sure you know the location of the designated rescue assistance area. Be sure that this area and all accessible routes are kept clear of book trucks, furniture, cleaning supplies, etc. It may only take a minute to move a book truck, but in an emergency, that minute may be too long to wait.
- Talk to your emergency coordinator. Find out what your responsibilities would be in a fire or other emergency. If you have any concerns about your duties or any limitations which would prevent you from performing them, let the coordinator know so that alternate plans are in place before a crisis occurs.
- If you will be expected to assist in evacuating people with disabilities, be sure you have the proper training. If you do not, or if your training is not up to date, let your supervisor know. Proper training is needed to protect the library, the patron, and you from both liability and injury.
- Keep abreast of changes in personnel which may affect staff members' responsibilities in an emergency. Know at all times who the emergency coordinator for your location is.
- Know the location of the emergency kit. If you must take any supplies from the kit, let the emergency coordinator know so that the supplies can be replaced.
- If your library conducts fire drills, take them seriously. Help coordinators analyze the effectiveness of procedures by pointing out the strengths and weaknesses of the drill.

Fire Drills and People with Disabilities

The tendency to dismiss fire alarms as false may actually work in favor of smooth building evacuation, because it makes people less likely to panic when they hear the alarm.

Ideally, fire drills should be unannounced, but in practice employees may have advance word of the drills. Never tell patrons "it's only a drill," even if you are certain that it is. The likelihood of an actual emergency occurring at the same time as a scheduled drill is extremely remote, but it does exist. Dismissing the alarm as unimportant undermines the purpose of the drill and endangers staff members and patrons.

In libraries where prank fire alarm calls are frequent, people may clump around uncertainly when the fire bell sounds, unwilling to stop working or studying until the emergency is verified. It is up to employees to combat this tendency and treat every alarm as though it is the real thing. Time is of the essence in an emergency, and waiting around may cause injury or even cost lives.

IN AN EMERGENCY

- Remain calm.
- Check the building and be sure that all patrons are aware of the emergency and understand the evacuation procedure.
- Be sure that hearing-impaired patrons know an emergency exists. If you are responsible for clearing the building, check every room, including all rest rooms, to make sure everybody is aware of the emergency. To get the attention of a hearing-impaired individual, stand in front of the patron, rap on the table, or tap the patron lightly on the shoulder.
- If a patron has a disability, explain the evacuation procedure, then ask the patron how you may be of assistance.
- If the emergency involves evacuating an upper floor, assist patrons using wheelchairs to the designated area of rescue assistance and wait with them until help arrives. DO NOT LEAVE PATRONS ALONE.
- If safety conditions require evacuating the stairwell and the wheelchair is small and light enough, the patron may be carried down in the wheelchair. If the wheelchair is too heavy to move, ask the patron for the best way to transfer him or her from the wheelchair. Use an evacuation sling, sturdy chair, or two-arm lock position to carry the patron down the stairs and out of the building. Designate someone to remain with the patron until the emergency is over.
- Assist semi-ambulatory patrons to facilitate rapid evacuation and to ensure they are not knocked over by other evacuees. The patrons and a designated person should wait for help in the area of rescue assistance. Designate someone to bring out any mobility aid the patron may be using.
- Offer your elbow to guide visually impaired patrons to the stairwell. Although people with visual impairments will need little guidance after reaching the exit stairwell, follow these patrons down the exit stairs to prevent their being pushed down from behind in the event of crowd-

Never carry someone out of the building except as a last resort. Stay with anyone who cannot negotiate stairs at the area of rescue assistance and wait for help. Carrying people can injure both the people being carried and the ones who are lifting.

If you are uncomfortable or unfamiliar with evacuation techniques, contact your local Red Cross office. They should be able to give you a schedule of their training classes and may even be willing to schedule on-site training for library staff members.

Form a chain!

If you have an injured person or someone who needs assistance in a large building, form a human chain to the door to help rescuers find the person as quickly as possible. The first person remains with the person who needs help, then the rest of the people fan out toward the exit. Each "link" in the chain stays within eyesight of the people before and after. The last person in the chain should stand where the emergency vehicles will arrive. When help does arrive, emergency workers can follow the chain to its source without having to worry about getting lost. The chain members can also allow the people at the area where help is needed to communicate with others without having to leave the person who needs aid.

ing. Designate a staff member to remain with patrons until the emergency is over.

• Ask any individuals with motor control disabilities due to brain, spinal, or nerve injury or other mental impairments how you can best be of assistance. If the patron uses a mobility aid or wheelchair or cannot negotiate stairs, escort the patron to the area of rescue assistance. Designate a staff member to wait with the patron until help arrives or the emergency is over.

• Individuals with temporary disabilities resulting from injuries or a condition which causes functional limitations should be asked to tell staff members about any special needs. People who cannot negotiate stairs should be taken to the area of rescue assistance, where a designated staff member should remain until help arrives or the emergency is over.

Liability Vs. Responsibility

Staff members may be reluctant to provide aid to patrons with disabilities out of a fear of doing more harm than good. This is a valid fear and is why the staff member should simply get the patron to the nearest area of rescue assistance and wait for help to arrive.

Some situations, however, may demand immediate action. Many states have "Good Samaritan" laws which absolve rescuers from liability when they are trying to save a life. If this is not the case, library managers should check with the local government or institution's safety department or the local Red Cross or fire department for guidelines on assisting patrons in emergency situations without incurring liability for staff members. Library managers should share the guidelines with staff members, who must be sure they understand what they should and should not do.

CONCLUSION

Safety issues should be placed foremost in any effort to serve patrons with disabilities. Preparation for an emergency does not take much time or expense, and can very literally save lives. Libraries which neglect safety concerns in their plans are, in a word, playing with fire.

Staff members who gain understanding and knowledge of how best to aid people with disabilities in an emergency can save lives. This fact alone should be sufficient reason to encourage library managers to develop and practice safety procedures which will anticipate and prevent the unique problems associated with assisting people with disabilities in emergencies.

RESOURCES

Americans with Disabilities Act Handbook. Equal Employment Opportunity Commission and the U.S. Department of Justice, October 1991. EEOC-BK-19

This handbook provides text of the Americans with Disabilities Act of 1990, interpretations, and ADA Accessibility Guidelines for Buildings and Facilities. Using this source will help you to determine whether your accommodations are appropriate and safe for people with disabilities.

Systems and Procedures Exchange Center. *Library Services for Persons with Disabilities*. SPEC Kit 176. Washington, D.C.: Association of Research Libraries, 1991.

Building evacuation procedures of four university libraries are provided. One caveat: the University of Texas procedure (p. 80) recommends carrying a person in his or her wheelchair or, if this is not possible, moving the person to an area of rescue assistance only after ambulatory persons have been evacuated. As noted in the text, it is dangerous to both patrons and staff members to carry people, and this should not be done except in a dire emergency. Because time is of the essence in an emergency, we also disagree with the recommendation that non-ambulatory patrons be asked to wait unassisted until others have been evacuated. They should be escorted to an area of rescue assistance as quickly as possible.

SUBJECT INDEX

AUTHOR/TITLE INDEX

Courtney Deines-Jones is a librarian for East Baton Rouge Parish Library. In addition to providing reference, circulation, and children's services at a downtown branch, she coordinates Americans with Disabilities Act compliance efforts for the system, which includes a main library and eleven branches. Ms. Deines-Jones received her MLIS and CLIS from Louisiana State University, where she was a Title II-B Fellow specializing in services to patrons with disabilities. She has written and lectured on various aspects of library service provision in the United States and Canada, focusing on the implications of emerging electronic technologies.

Connie Van Fleet (MLIS, Ph.D.) is Associate Professor, School of Library and Information Science, Louisiana State University and the recipient of the 1995 LSU University Excellence in Teaching Award. With the support of USDE Title II-B Library and Education awards, she developed the school's first course in library and information services to people with disabilities. She is a frequent contributor to the library and information science literature and an active speaker at professional meetings on the state and national levels. Dr. Van Fleet is co-editor of *RQ*, journal of the Reference and Adult Services Division of the American Library Association, and is President of the Patrons of the East Baton Rouge Parish Library.

Typography: Network Typesetting, Inc.
Cover: Apicella Design